Treats for your
DOG

Treats for your
DOG

HOW TO PAMPER YOUR POOCH:
PRACTICAL PROJECTS TO PROVE YOU CARE,
WITH OVER 400 PHOTOGRAPHS

PHOTOGRAPHY BY
JANE BURTON

LORENZ BOOKS

This edition is published by Lorenz Books
an imprint of Anness Publishing Ltd
Blaby Road, Wigston
Leicestershire LE18 4SE
info@anness.com

www.lorenzbooks.com
www.annesspublishing.com

If you like the images in this book and would like
to investigate using them for publishing, promotions or advertising,
please visit our website www.practicalpictures.com for more information.

© Anness Publishing Ltd 2013

A CIP catalogue record for this book is available from the British Library.

Publisher: Joanna Lorenz
Senior Editor: Clare Nicholson
Consultant: Trevor Turner B.Vet. Med. M.R.C.V.S.
Special Photography: Jane Burton
Designers: Peter Butler and Susannah Good
Illustrator: Jane Molineaux
Production Controller: Mai-Ling Collyer

PUBLISHER'S NOTE
Although the advice and information in this book are believed to be accurate and true at the time
of going to press, neither the authors nor the publisher can accept any legal responsibility or liability
for any errors or omissions that may have been made nor for any inaccuracies nor for any loss,
harm or injury that comes about from following instructions or advice in this book.

CONTENTS

Introduction

When everyone else is being beastly, isn't it good to know that there's *someone* who'll give you their unswerving loyalty and affection? Who'll snuggle up close to you for a hug and a kiss no matter how dreadful the day has been?

Yes, that's why you're a dog-owner. To modify the cliché, a pooch is a person's best pal. A pooch will love you selflessly and endlessly when all the rest of the world seems to have abandoned you to your fate. Not any old pooch, of course: *your* Pooch, the one and only.

If your devoted dog is prepared to stick with you at times of stress, don't you think you ought to be prepared to pamper your pet all the rest of the time? Shouldn't a dog's life be the best of all possible lives?

This is the ultimate dog care manual – a lifestyle book, an inspirational guide-to-living, a cookbook, a craft book, and the only book your pet will care about you owning.

House Your Hound In Style

All dogs are remarkably sensitive to their surroundings. Playfulness and natural ruggedness aside, they are essentially houseproud. So, even if you prefer a simple lifestyle, and your own home falls some

way short of luxurious, there is no reason why your companion's special areas should be anything less than comfortable and beautifully designed. Big or small, young or old, your dog will want to live somewhere that has style. So do invest time and effort in your friend's accommodation: it's the least you can give in return for the unbounded love he will offer you.

Without a beautiful abode, being a beast is just a burden. So keep your pet in stately style and construct a canine castle, complete with eaves and finials, and painted in his favourite colours.

For a companion with slightly more inflated ideas, who leans a little towards the past for design inspiration, a Taj Mahal theme could provide the kennel of his dreams.

All Mod Kens

Top dogs deserve the best, and cold old kennels just won't do. Whether a pooch palace for sophisticated urbanites or a rural cottage idyll for country dogs, this is the guide to creating the doghouse of pet dreams.

Like the best architects and interior designers, you will want to consult your pet as to their own preferences before fixing upon the new dog decor. Personality, style, taste and comfort requirements will all direct your choice of decoration. Remember, a kennel is your pet's castle: it is much more than just a place to sleep, ruminate, or hide a bone: it is somewhere he can be private with his own thoughts and preserve his independence in a dog-eat-dog world.

For the three-dog family this ingenious construction provides all the answers, and its top can also be used by friends as a day couch or general lounger.

Fresh and fun, this witty kennel design is for dogs with panache and an appreciation of art.

De Chirico Kennel

Clever use of paint perspective – inspired by the well-known twentieth-century painter De Chirico – transforms an everyday abode into a dream den.

You will need:

kennel • acrylic paints in blue, black, white, and burnt umber • a range of paintbrushes • protective gloves • piece of tin • metal cutters • sandpaper • hammer • children's windmill toy • strong adhesive • short length of wire • craft knife • nail

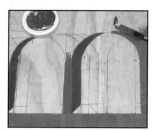

1 Paint the kennel, and on each side paint four arches receding in height. Wearing gloves, cut a cockerel and an arrow out of tin. Sand any rough edges and hammer flat.

2 Then paint the cockerel. Attach to a windmill toy with wire and glue.

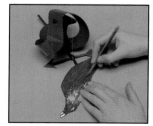

3 Scratch off some of the paint and nail the weathervane to the roof.

Folk-art Kennel

The essence of folk style is its naive quality, of course, so don't worry if your painting skills are on the primitive side.

You will need:

kennel • yellow oil paint • linseed oil • white spirit • sponge or rag • ruler and pencil • jar • a range of paintbrushes, including a stencil brush • acrylic paints in red, blue, green and black • tracing paper • thin card • craft knife • sandpaper • strip of tin for roof • metal cutters • protective gloves • clear varnish • 5mm (¼in) nails

2 Enlarge the template of the urn from page 92 and draw it onto thin card. Cut it out. Place the stencil in the centre of a panel, hold firmly and stencil in blue paint. Repeat on each panel.

3 Use a 5mm (¼in) brush to paint leaf shapes, applying more pressure at the end of the stroke, thus achieving a curving line that tapers at one end. Paint roses and tulips in broad, thick strokes. Allow to dry, and then define petal lines with a fine brush.

4 Outline the panels in black paint, and if you prefer a slightly aged effect use sandpaper to distress the paint finish. Then paint the inside of the kennel blue.

5 To decorate the roof, cut a strip of tin the length of the kennel by 30cm (12in) (wear protective gloves). Fold in half lengthways then cut a zigzag edge along the long sides. Sand down and rub yellow oil paint into the metal, until no excess paint is on the surface. Varnish to seal. When dry nail to the roof.

Any rural dog would appreciate this gorgeous country home in vernacular decorative style.

1 Mix some yellow oil paint with one part linseed and two parts white spirit. Rub it into the wood with a sponge or rag. With a ruler, measure out panels on the sides of the kennel. To create the inverted curves on the corners, draw around a jar. Paint the borders red.

Transports of Delight

Some dogs love travelling, especially by car; others make a fuss from the moment you leave the house until you reach your destination. If your dog is one of the latter, you can at least offer the compensation of a carrier that is individualistic and deliciously comfortable – custom-made, and fashioned with care and affection. These stylish designs are for dogs on the move, and are guaranteed to turn every trip into an event. Walking the dog just won't be the same.

Plain cardboard pet carriers are always a useful and cheap option – but there is no reason why they can't be transformed as transporters. Use decoupage, stencilling or stamping to create beautiful repeat patterns and devices; or, as here, transform them into trompe l'oeil coaches.

South American Bus Dog Carrier

Inspired by South American painted buses, this is for the dog that is truly going places.

You will need:

cardboard pet carrier • cardboard • ruler • scissors • craft knife • masking tape • newspaper • PVA glue • acrylic paints: green, blue, red, yellow, black and white • paintbrush • scraps of coloured paper

2 Attach this box to the front of the carrier. Then papier-mâché the box by dipping strips of newspaper in diluted PVA glue. When dry, repeat with a second layer. Cut out four circles for the wheels and bind them to the box with papier-mâché.

1 To make the bumper, cut a piece of cardboard the width of the front of the carrier and about 13cm (5in) deep, adding a margin of 2.5cm (1in) all around. Lightly score along the margin and fold these flaps up. Using masking tape, stick the corners together to make a shallow box.

3 Paint the sides, roof and handles, and paint doors, windows and passengers on the bus in bright primary colours. Highlight particular features such as the door and bumper by sticking on strips of coloured paper.

Fur-rari Racer

The ultimate recycling project – take an old pram frame, drawer and a cardboard box and create this car which will put your dog in first place. The drawer must fit on the pram frame so that the wheels can move freely.

You will need:

drawer • red and white acrylic paint • a range of paintbrushes • two nails • hammer • three pipe clips and screws • screwdriver • old pram frame • cardboard box to fit over drawer • marker pen • craft knife • adhesive • large sheet of polyester board or cardboard • pins • yellow tape

1 Paint the drawer red. Knock two nails into the front and back: these will support the box. Then position the three clips on the drawer so that they clip onto the frame. Place the drawer over the frame and clip on.

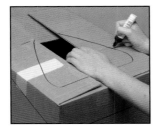

2 Push the bottom flaps of the box up inside. On the top mark out the cockpit. Draw a sloping line on one side of the box, along the front and up the other side. This will form a hinged lid. Cut along these lines.

5 The side panels can be cut from cardboard or polyester board. Paint them red and glue them to the box. Make the eyes from polyester board. Then paint them and glue them on the bumper a small distance from the front of the box so that the hinged lid can be slotted in behind them and held firmly in place.

3 Cut down the corners of the hinged lid and bring the flap that is now free about 2cm (¾in) out, then glue it in place. This will allow the lid to close sloping down. Paint the box red.

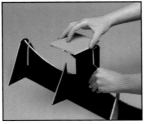

6 On the back of the box, make a slot for the spoiler out of polyester board. Then make the spoiler in the same way as the bumper.

4 Cut the main bumper out of polyester board. The central indents should be the same width as the front of the box. Make the support which will hold the bumper on and cut out two arrow shapes. Pin the pieces together while the adhesive dries. Then glue the bumper onto the support. Paint the bumper red and add yellow tape to highlight it. Fix the bumper to the box.

All revved up and raring to go.

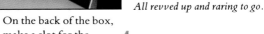

Baskets of Distinction

Unless your dog is extremely unusual, statistics indicate that he will spend a lot of time in bed – day-dreaming, thinking, or even actually sleeping. The hours and rigorous discipline invested in these pastimes should be recognized by the provision of really special sleeping accommodation.

A certain kind of dog – and you will know if you have one – prefers stylish restraint to anything too "soft" or cosy. These clean lines are complemented by stark colouring – the essence of minimalist chic.

Wicker is traditional, homely, airy and healthy – always a safe choice. But don't forget it is also hard, cold in winter, and can have jagged edges – so line any wicker basket with an old blanket.

Canine Castle

Cardboard boxes make ideal dog baskets, and with a little adjustment they can be turned into fantastic palaces, such as this castle – though don't expect them to last long if your hound is at all destructive.

You will need:

large cardboard box • marker pen • ruler • craft knife • strong tape • acrylic paints: blue, yellow, black and red • a range of paintbrushes • two lengths of fine chain • thin wire • polyester board • strong adhesive • masking tape • yellow tape

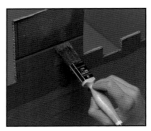

2 Carefully cut out all the sections. It may be a good idea to strengthen the box with strong tape and folded cardboard struts in the corners. Then paint the box blue, both inside and out. When dry, paint bone motifs on the side and front of the box. Then outline the bones with black paint.

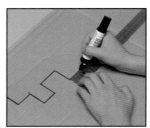

1 Mark out castellations around the sides of the box, leaving the corners and a section in the middle of the back edge their original height. Also leave a plain section in the front for the drawbridge.

3 Cut the drawbridge out of the front of the box and then pierce holes in the four corners for the chains to go through. Secure the chains with wire.

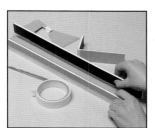

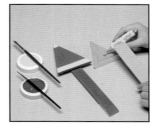

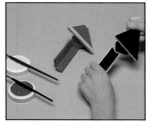

4 For each of the tall flagpoles on the back, cut three rectangles about 50 × 5cm (20 × 2in) from polyester board. Lay one of these on the work surface, then glue a rectangle on each edge. To make the back support, cut two rectangles of board which will form an L-shape. They should be narrow enough to slot inbetween the flagpoles and deep enough to stand out from the back (see step 5). Cut out a triangle and flag.

5 Stick the flag to the back of the triangle and position it as shown, then glue in place. Slot the back support in between the back of the flagpoles: it should stand out from the back and be level with the base. Paint the flagpoles blue and decorate with yellow tape. Paint the flags red and decorate with bones.

6 Make the two front turrets as shown. The support on the back of the triangle will allow the triangle to hang over the box while the pole goes down the back. Decorate as before.

7 Make the two turrets for the back corners of the box so that the supports fit around the corner, and the triangle will hang over the front. Decorate as before.

8 Make the central keep so that it slots over the back panel of the box. Paint on windows and decorate with tape. Glue in position.

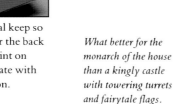

What better for the monarch of the house than a kingly castle with towering turrets and fairytale flags.

Soft Furnishings

Complementary and well-integrated soft furnishings – cushions, covers and curtains – are an essential element of any well-planned interior. Here you have two aspects to consider: firstly, appropriate and robust furnishings specifically for your dog and his possessions, probably with particularly canine themes such as bones and balls; and secondly, sympathetic styling throughout your own large-scale decor because your friend shares it, too.

This terrier can snooze and dream of roaming the range on a cowhide daybed. The fur is fake and functional: synthetics such as this will prove extra hard-wearing.

Use sturdy material for this cushion, because even the cutest of puppies have sharp teeth and a tendency to chew the immediate environment.

Good, durable fabrics for dog furnishings are jute, hessian, corduroy, denim, and any upholstery fabrics recommended for chairs and sofas.

This striking appliqué cushion has dalmation-style polka dots stitched on in felt – one side in classic black and white colour-way, the other in racy pink and orange.

Canine Curtain

Your dog will sometimes appreciate a little privacy when washing or feeding – and this delightful dog-pattern appliqué curtain (which could also be fashioned as a screen) is the perfect answer.

You will need:

tracing paper • soft pencil • thin card • scraps of fabric for dogs and circles • bondaweb • scissors • fabric for curtain • 10 × 20cm (4 × 8in) lengths of ribbon • needle and matching thread • pins

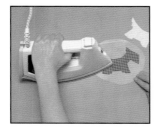

2 Peel the paper off the bondaweb and iron the Scottie dog onto a circle of contrasting fabric.

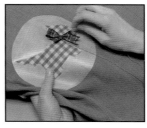

3 Iron bondaweb onto the reverse of the fabric circles and iron them onto the curtain. Sew a ribbon onto each dog.

4 Evenly place the ribbon ties on the right side of the fabric along the top edge and place a flap of fabric over. Pin together and sew along the edge to secure the ribbons. Turn the flap to the wrong side, and hem the side seams and bottom edge.

1 Using the pattern on page 92, make a template of the Scottie dog. Iron bondaweb onto the reverse of the fabric you are going to use for the dogs and draw round the template. Cut out the shape.

The curtain going up on a really gorgeous little production! You know your companion, so use his or her favourite motifs and colour schemes to customize the design. The basic pattern can be adapted and personalized for any type of dog with a little creative thought and imagination.

In the Home

Your dog may seem oblivious to his surroundings (other than knowing the comfiest seat or most awkward spot to lie in), but dogs are highly conscious of good design and decor, and have a distinct sense of style and taste. This varies considerably from breed to breed, but as an owner you will be more than aware of your own companion's personal preferences, and favourite decorating devices and embellishments.

Think about design schemes that will delight and excite your friend. This succulent meat repeat is made by photocopying the motifs for decoupage against a strong background.

This "lead tidy" is simply made from a piece of wood cut into a bone shape. Here dowelling is used for the hangers, but you can just as easily screw in hooks.

Treat Chest

Make (or buy secondhand and embellish) a "Treat Chest" to hold all of your dog's favourite toys, accessories and special possessions.

You will need:

sandpaper • chest or cupboard • emulsion paints • paintbrushes • tracing paper • soft pencil • thin card • MDF wood (0.5cm/¼in thick) • fret saw • strong adhesive • gemstones • clear varnish •

Any chest can be painted, in any number of ways: why not try bones, paw prints and balls.

1 Sandpaper the chest then paint it in your chosen colours. Using the template on page 92, paint bones and spots around the frame.

2 From MDF wood cut a dog bone for the handle and cut in half. Sand the edges. Paint the bone and glue on an assortment of gemstones. Varnish the bone. Glue the bone handle onto the door knobs so that the two pieces meet together. Leave the glue to harden before using.

Photo Frame

A photograph of your best friend in the world cannot help but be enhanced if you make a specially designed frame for it. This effect can be created with collage, decoupage or mosaic – or more simply with paint effects.

You will need:

corrugated cardboard • pencil • scissors • PVA glue • glue spreader • wallpaper paste • strips of newspaper 2cm (¾in) long • ready-mixed tile grout • knife for applying grout • novelty toys or broken pieces of china for decoration • gold acrylic paint • paintbrush •

1 Cut out two heart shapes the same size from corrugated cardboard. Cut a smaller heart shape out of the centre of one of the hearts. Also cut out one right-angled triangle and one equilateral triangle from cardboard.

2 Stick the right-angled triangle vertically to the complete heart, so that the right angle is at the tip of the base of the heart. Centre the equilateral triangle on the right-angled one and stick it in place. Mix up a small quantity of wallpaper paste and saturate the strips of newspaper in it. Paste the strips onto the hearts and triangles until they are well covered then leave to dry.

If your companion has a special friend or absent loved one, this makes the perfect gift for his basket-side. But most owners are going to keep this for themselves, containing a favourite studio portrait of their one and only: it is particularly appropriate for the lonely room of the business traveller, and is bound to gain the respect and sympathy of hotel staff all over the world.

3 To decorate the frame, apply ready-mixed grout to the heart outline and embed novelty toys or broken china in it. Allow to dry for 24 hours.

4 Paint the back of the frame with gold paint and then paint in between the objects on the outline heart. When dry, stick the frame to the backing heart, leaving the top open to slip your doggy photo into the frame.

On the Dogwalk

Some dogs are naturally and instinctively elegant and, for these, personal embellishment is a joy. Other breeds are more down to earth and therefore a little shyer about fashion, and a little more modest about display. However, all dogs have innate character and poise, and just need very slight encouragement to push them into the world of glamour. With imagination and flair you can create amazing accessories for your hirsute hound – smart evening coats, woolly winter jackets, chic collars, robust neckerchiefs and many more outfits to set your pet off to perfection.

Modesty is only fur-deep, and the natural show-off that lurks within your dog needs only a little encouragement to come out and play. This Superdog just loves being caught in the spotlight.

This fleecy little coat is both warm and chic, and therefore ideal for smart urban dogs who make occasional trips to the countryside.

Overdogs

Your dog's own coat is of course the most stylish and beautiful of all. However, what better way to keep the rain off, to keep the cold out, and add a splash of colour or a dash of flair on a *really* special occasion, than a delightful personalized covering designed by you?

This "sports" cut coat leaves plenty of room for leg movement.

Creating a splash in the most racy of raincoats: sunshine yellow is the way to go when all around is grey.

Knitted Coat

For a gayer, less formal look on a cold day, this knitted overcoat with contrasting patch and appliqué device (in this instance, a bone) is witty, yet functional.

1 Follow the knitting pattern on page 93. Then to make up the coat, gently press all pieces. Using the palest green Aran weight yarn, chain stitch the bone outline inside the pink stomach area.

This chunky knit is perfect for keeping your pet pal warm on those frosty winter walks.

You will need:

pair of size 6 (4.5mm) needles • 100g (4 oz skein) turquoise (T) Aran weight yarn • small amounts of pink (P) and palest green aran weight yarn • large darning needle • turquoise sewing thread • sewing needle • 4 turquoise 2cm (¾in) buttons • tape measure • scissors

2 Sew in all ends. Sew two buttons on the neck strap. Sew the other two either side of the coat on the garter stitch trim area 8cm (3¼in) from the back edge.

Classic Tartan

This classic tartan overcoat with black ribbon tie is, of course, the basis of any terrier's wardrobe.

You will need:

paper for pattern • pencil • scissors • 30cm × 115cm (12 × 45in) tartan fabric • 30 × 115cm (12in × 45in) wadding • 30cm × 115cm (12in × 45in) lining • pins • needle and matching thread • velcro fastenings • bias binding • satin ribbon

2 Lay the patterns on top of the layers of fabric once again and trim.

3 Sew the velcro fastenings on the stomach piece.

4 Join the two side pieces together along the back. Pin and sew on the bias binding. Make a bow out of satin ribbon, and sew onto the front together with the velcro fastenings for the chest.

Cutting a Highland dash in smart tartan – perfect for spring and autumn when there is a nip in the air.

1 Using the template on page 92 as a guide, scale up and cut out paper patterns for the right and left sides. Place on the tartan fabric and cut out, making sure that the tartan lines will match across the centre back seam. Cut out the wadding and lining slightly larger. Pin and tack the top, wadding and lining together. Quilt along the tartan patterning.

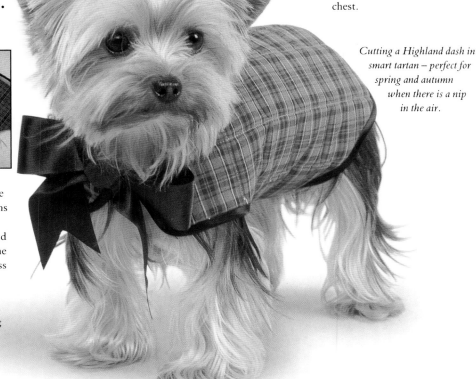

Accessory Heaven

The coat isn't the end of the fashion story, of course: there are complementary accoutrements that the well-dressed dog-about-town will need as standard. Hats – to fend off the rain – are a start, and a scarf is always practical. On a summer evening, by contrast, your companion's thoughts will turn from the functional towards simple self-adornment – perhaps with something as simple as a fancy bow tie.

This flamboyant piece of neckwear would also look spectacular with painted spots, stripes or even paw prints.

Bow Tie

Add a splash of colour to your pampered pooch with this bow tie, which simply fastens onto your dog's collar. You can scale the measurements up and down to suit your dog.

You will need:

30 × 30cm (12 × 12in) white cotton fabric • small embroidery hoop • soft pencil • gold-coloured gutta or outliner pen • fabric paints: red, green, yellow, lilac, blue, orange and brown • scissors • 20 × 20cm (8 × 8in) purple cotton fabric • pins • needle and matching threads • small piece of velcro

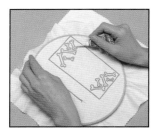

1 Fasten the white fabric into the hoop. Using a soft pencil mark out a rectangle 7.5 × 14cm (3 × 5½in) for the bow and another 10 × 3.75cm (4 × 1½in) for the central band. Leave room for seam allowances between the rectangles. Draw on a pattern then paint over with the gold outliner pen and leave to dry.

2 Using the fabric paints, fill in the shapes with your chosen colours. Colour just outside the rectangles too. When dry, cut out the rectangles, leaving a 1.5cm (⅝in) seam allowance. Then cut rectangles to the same size from the purple fabric.

3 Fold the edges under 1.5cm (⅝in) on the painted fabric and 1.25cm (½in) on the purple onto the wrong side. Pin the two rectangles together, wrong sides facing, and sew them together. Repeat for the central band.

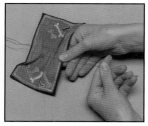

4 Sew two rows of gathering threads along the centre of the bow. Gather to make it approximately 2.5cm (1in) deep. Sew the central band to the gathered bow tie with machine or hand stitches.

5 Finally, sew velcro to the central bands at either end to finish. Fasten to a dog's collar.

Winter Woolly

For a winter walk, sledding with the lads or that unexpected invitation to Gstaad – this stylish monogrammed woolly hat makes a strong statement anytime, anywhere.

You will need:

50g (2 oz skein) red aran weight yarn • pair of size 6 (4.5mm) needles • small amount of white Aran weight yarn • large darning needle • scissors • cardboard

1 Follow the knitting pattern on page 93. Then make up the hat. Using the white yarn, embroider an initial on the front of the hat between the two ear holes.

2 Pull the thread running through the last row of stitches to gather up the top of the hat. Sew up the back seam and sew in all ends.

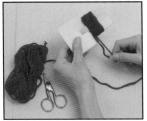

3 To make the pompom, cut a piece of card to wrap the wool around. Wind the red yarn around the card until the yarn is 3.75cm (1½in) deep. Tie a piece of yarn tightly around the centre of the pompom. Cut the yarn either side of the card to release the pompom.

4 Trim until the pompom is neat and round. Sew the pompom onto the top of the hat.

A scarf in the shape of a bone is nice warm wear for a cold day, and inspires pleasant thoughts of a good chew by the hearth at the end of it. A scarf with a cat is even tastier.

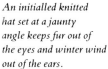

An initialled knitted hat set at a jaunty angle keeps fur out of the eyes and winter wind out of the ears.

Party Wear

Social occasions, special events and celebrations call for a little more sophistication. Here are some simple but highly effective ideas that will make a striking impression whatever the gathering and whatever the competition.

Certainly not for serious wear, but to make an entrance at any party you need look no further than these flamboyant sunglasses.

Sunglasses

Adapt a pair of old sunglasses to give your pet the full film-star look.

You will need:

wire • adhesive • cheap plastic sunglasses • glue spreader • wallpaper paste • strips of newspaper 2.5cm (1in) wide • red acrylic paint • paintbrush • gold paint • jewels

Evening elegance with a sumptous ensemble in rich red and seed pearls. Very chic, very Dogue.

1 Twist two pieces of wire to provide a frame for the shape you want the glasses to be. Stick the wire onto the glasses.

2 Mix up the wallpaper paste and saturate the pieces of newspaper in it. Stick them to the glasses, avoiding the lenses and arms.

3 Paint the glasses red then leave to dry.

4 Decorate with gold paint and stick on jewels.

Evening Outfit

This stylish coat will suit any dog who wants to hit the town.

You will need:

paper for pattern • soft pencil • scissors • 1m (1yd) × 115cm (45in) black cotton fabric • 0.5m (½yd) of 50g (2oz) polyester wadding • safety pins • pins • needle and matching thread • scrap of interlining and lurex fabric • bias binding • decorative buttons • hook and eye • silver ribbon • buckle and catch

1 Using the template on page 92 as a guide, scale up and cut out a paper pattern for the coat. Cut out a square of black fabric large enough to take the pattern.

2 Cut the wadding and a second square of black fabric for the backing, slightly larger than the first. Safety pin all the layers together.

3 Then machine or hand quilt (see page 94). Remove the safety pins, lay the pattern on top and pin, then cut out the coat. Sew a small dart into the centre at the tail end of the coat.

For fancy dress parties or Christmas day, dress your dog so that it is the belle of the ball.

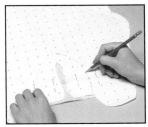

4 Iron the interlining onto the lurex fabric. Mark the area of the neckline on the pattern, as shown, then place the pattern on top of the lurex fabric and cut out the marked area.

5 Place the lurex fabric over the coat and turn back the collar. Pin to the coat at the neck and sew into place, covering the raw edges with bias binding. Cut bias strips from the lurex fabric and sew them around the rest of the coat. Sew decorative buttons over the surface of the coat and also buttons to hold back the lapel collar. Sew on a hook and eye as the front fastener.

6 Cut a strip of black cotton fabric 0.5m × 5cm (18 × 2in) wide and sew to form a belt. Sew silver ribbon down the centre and on one end place the buckle. Sew on to the centre of the back and sew a catch at the side of the coat.

Canine Collars

No self-respecting dog would ever be seen outside without a collar, yet it's surprising how little attention most owners are prepared to pay to such an essential accessory. Every dog needs a wide range of collars: formal wear; informal; sports wear; party style; casual; lounging and so on. When choosing or designing canine collars, think first about your companion's colouring, personal style, physical make-up and other characteristics. Choose accessories that will complement and emphasize your friend's finest qualities.

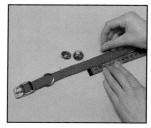

A country-style bandana for a rural dog.

Officer Dog Collar

You can easily decorate any dog collar to suit the style of your hound. This classy collar is for any dog which has to go on parade.

You will need:

standard dog collar • pins • tape measure • needle and matching thread • gold buttons • scissors • gold braid

1 Mark where the buttons are to be sewn on with pins. Use a tape measure to get the spacing very even.

2 Sew on the buttons firmly and then cut a length of gold braid and sew it on too.

Every dog looks dashing in uniform – there's nothing like a bit of gold braid at the neck to impress.

Sometimes the simplest approach makes the strongest statement: a classic band in bottle-green for a smart country-chic look.

Jewelled Collar

To make this eye-catching collar, take a plain off-the-shelf model, use a dash of spray paint and embellish with diamanté.

You will need:

corrugated cardboard 2.5cm (1in) wide and long enough to go around your dog's neck • two pieces of wire 3.75cm (1½in) long • adhesive • glue spreader • wallpaper paste • newspaper strips 2.5cm (1in) wide • gold acrylic paint • paintbrush • 0.5m (½yd) ribbon • jewels for decoration

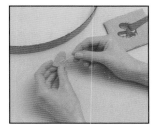

1 Cut a small heart out of corrugated cardboard. Bend one piece of the wire into a U-shape and stick it in the middle of the collar. Stick the other piece straight onto the heart.

2 Mix up a quantity of wallpaper paste and saturate the newspaper strips in it. Stick two layers of papier-mâché onto the collar, easing the collar into a curved shape.

3 Paint both the collar and the heart gold. Then stick the ribbon ties onto each end of the collar.

4 Stick jewels on the collar and heart. Loop the wire on the heart through the loop on the collar and bend backwards to lie flat.

Wearing a heart on his neck rather than on his sleeve – a razzle-dazzle band in highly contemporary style.

Leather and studs are a centuries-old convention in dogwear, but can be continually varied and updated for freshness. The one constant is the effect created – a hint of machismo.

Canine Cuisine

Y ou only have to look at the expectantly
    wagging tail and the bright eyes of a healthy
dog to know that feeding is one of the greatest
pleasures in his life. This vital section is on how to
create unforgettable meals that will thrill your
companion's taste buds. Moving far beyond pet
food, this
chapter is about
"food for the
dogs". The way
to a pet's heart
is undoubtedly
through its
stomach: your
dog's senses of

taste and scent are far more developed than our
own, so it seems quite unfair to bore him with
mass-produced fare. These delectable recipes
guarantee happier, healthier pets – from doggy
chews to savoury stews, this is the food your
four-legged friend will favour.

Every dog hides a gourmet under the gourmand exterior, and tempting treats are a sure way to strengthen the bond between you. In this chapter are recipes for all occasions – haute-cuisine recipes to entice and delight, special low-fat dishes (for the more sedentary pet), nutritious get-up-and-go morsels and delectable doggie savouries.

Your pooch may pretend to show equal zeal for whatever is served up in his dog bowl, but don't be fooled: quality cuisine served up with love and attention will always be appreciated.

TV Snacks and Titbits

It's the little things in life that make a difference, and it's the little "just because I love you" treats that will cheer up your pet's day. These are perfect TV snacks, light lunches and brunches, with a couple of healthy low-fat options thrown in for those who have a heavy walk ahead of them (or a heavy dinner planned that evening). These are dishes you can whisk up in a trice, while the title credits to "Lassie" are still rolling up on the screen.

Remember that any snacks you give your friend are part of an overall diet: take them into account when you're assessing their overall intake.

Make treating your pet a conscious decision, and try not to leave edibles on show: this pup still has to learn the art of disguise regarding ad-hoc snacking, but he'll be a master before too long.

Raw Goodness

This surprising treat is perhaps the simplest of all recipes for a canine snack! Just top and tail one or more raw carrots, cut into smaller chunks if your dog is small, and present them to your pet. If he turns up his nose at the carrots, give them a light brush of animal fat or beef extracts. The carrot is a valuable source of vitamins as well as a popular crunchy goodie.

Eat up, they'll help you see in the dark

INSTANT SNACKS

Breakfast cereals with milk
Scrambled eggs
Plain boiled rice
Cooked pasta
Raw fruit and vegetables

Sentimental spicy sausage

Snappy Snacks

225g/8oz wholemeal flour
115g/4oz textured soya protein
(after steeping), mince
or sausagemeat

Preheat the oven to 180°C/350°F/ Gas 4. Put the flour in a bowl and mix with water until you've formed a nice paste. If using mince or soya protein, stir into the paste until thoroughly mixed; if using sausagemeat, put the paste into a blender or food processor, crumble in the sausagemeat, and process until the mixture looks even. Roll out the mixture to about 3mm/⅛in thick, and cut into bite-sized shapes. Put onto sheets of greaseproof paper and bake for about 20 minutes, checking every couple of minutes after the first 10 minutes or so: you want these biscuits to be hard but not burnt black. After removing from the oven, cool and serve.

Meaty morsels for good dogs

Bunnyburgers

115g/4oz diced rabbit
2 egg yolks
2.5ml/½ tsp flour
a little gravy (if required)

Boil some water in a pan, throw in
the diced rabbit, cook for about 20
minutes, testing from time to time,
and stop as soon as a sharp fork will
sink easily into one of the cubes. If
using a food processor or blender,
process the meat, egg yolks and flour
until well mixed but "chunky";
otherwise, cook the meat a little
longer, then mash it with the other
ingredients until you have a
"chunky" paste. Cool, and squash it
out using a rolling pin to a layer
about 3mm/⅛in thick. Cut into bite-
sized shapes – why not use a rabbit-
shaped pastry-cutter? – and grill for a
few minutes on all sides until hard.
Cool and serve.

Canine Coleslaw

1 large or 2 small carrots
50g/2oz white cabbage (or heart
of green cabbage)
30ml/2 tbsp plain yogurt

Chop or slice up the carrot(s) and
cabbage and put in a bowl. Stir in the
yogurt – enough to give the mixture
a nice consistency. Serve. Any that
isn't used can be stored for up to 24
hours in the fridge.

The healthy option

What a drag . . . an evening in with
nothing to do. Nobody loves me . . .

She loves me! And I have the proof
between my teeth . . .

DOG'S TIP
To make the coleslaw more tasty, add a
little melted lard or beef extract.

Meat, Poultry and Fish

If left to his own devices, your dog would probably be happy to subsist on raw meat, supplemented by other scrounged or scavenged foods. Many a dog wouldn't object to a diet comprising of your leftovers – so long as there were enough of them!

But your dog is special and deserves better. If you want to tell your dog that your love is deep and strong, an excellent method is to serve up, every week or so, something that will appeal to the gourmet lurking deep in your dog's heart. At the core of such dishes should be first-class protein in the form of meat, poultry or white fish.

Before deciding the quantities you wish to feed your dog, consider the fat content. Fat is not as harmful to dogs as it is to humans but it is a significant source of calories. Fat is the natural energy source for your dog and thus is the most palatable component of food. There are some general principles:

■ fish and poultry have comparatively little fat
■ expensive cuts of meat, like steak, do not rate too badly – especially if you trim off any surplus fat before feeding the meat to your dog
■ cheaper cuts of meat – like mince – tend to be much fattier
■ some forms of offal, notably heart, have very high fat contents

How Much?

Since dogs come in all shapes and sizes and with differing appetites, you will need to experiment to find out what is a sensible meal for your own dog.

Breakfast brunch

Kanine Kedgeree

150g/5oz cooked white fish
15ml/1 tbsp lard
115g/4oz cooked wholegrain rice
1 large egg
2 slices cucumber

Check the fish very carefully for bones: always do this before serving your dog any fish. Place the lard in a saucepan and when melted, stir in the rice. Crumble in the fish and egg, stirring vigorously. When the egg is cooked remove the pan from the heat and allow to cool. Garnish with cucumber.

Pâté de Foie Grrrr

175g/6oz beef, pig's or lamb's kidney
1 chicken liver
60–70ml/4 heaped tbsp wholemeal breadcrumbs, oatmeal or pulverized breakfast cereal
1 large egg

Preheat the oven to 180°C/350°F/Gas 4. Boil some water in a pan. Cut up the kidney and liver into smallish chunks and simmer for about 15 minutes until very tender. Drain off the water, leaving a little and retaining the meaty froth. Cool, and add the breadcrumbs, oatmeal, or breakfast cereal, stirring vigorously. Add the egg and mash until you have an even mix. Put everything in a food processor or blender and process for about 20 seconds. Put into a small casserole dish and bake, without a lid, for about 45 minutes, checking regularly to watch that the top doesn't burn. Cool completely, and serve.

Pooch pâté

Mince magic for dogs

Wuff Cuts

*175g/6oz best mince
or minced chicken
50g/2oz textured soya protein chunks,
steeped overnight
1 large egg
15ml/1 tbsp wholemeal breadcrumbs,
oatmeal or pulverized breakfast cereal
1 carrot, peeled and cut into
small chunks
2 or more cooked broccoli florets,
to garnish*

Blend the meat or chicken and textured soya protein with the egg and breadcrumbs, oatmeal or breakfast cereal. Fold in the carrot until the chunks are well distributed. Form the mixture into four patties and grill for about 10 minutes under a medium-hot grill, turning occasionally. Allow to cool, then serve garnished with the broccoli florets.

Oriental Chow

*25ml/1½ tbsp lard
50g/2oz cabbage, cut into thin strips
50g/2oz carrot, peeled and cut into
thin strips
½ green pepper, cut into coarse strips
(optional)
25g/1oz canned water chestnuts, quartered
175g/6oz cooked chicken, cut into
thin strips*

Heat the lard in a saucepan or wok, and add the vegetables, stirring briskly until the edges of the vegetables begin to brown. Mix in the cooked chicken, leave to cool, and serve.

Chinese-style chicken

Sausage Zingers

*30ml/2 tbsp lard
175g/6oz sausagemeat
1 large egg, beaten
45–55ml/3 heaped tbsp wholemeal
breadcrumbs or oatmeal
50g/2oz cooked rice, to serve*

This is really just a nice way of serving sausage! Heat the lard in a frying pan over a moderate heat. Cut the sausagemeat into rounds about 5mm/¼in thick and fry for about 1 minute on each side. Take them out, coat them in beaten egg and then in breadcrumbs or oatmeal, return to the frying pan and fry for a further 8 minutes, turning frequently until brown. Allow to cool, and serve on a bed of rice.

Sausage spectacular

Not By Meat Alone

Although your dog's diet should be essentially meat-orientated, other foods are equally important – aside from health concerns, they add the element of variety that is so essential if your companion is going to anticipate and enjoy mealtimes rather than just filling up with fuel.

The Vegetarian Option

While it shouldn't be a habit, there's no reason at all why occasional vegetarian meals can't form a diverting and stimulating part of your friend's diet. Here are some possibilities:

Tofu: Use in chunks wherever you might use chunks of meat. Tofu doesn't taste of anything very much, so make sure the rest of the meal is sufficiently rich in taste. Tofu has a wonderful capacity for picking up flavours from other foods and sauces.

Tasty tofu for health-conscious types

Textured Soya Protein: As noted in some of the recipes, this can be used in conjunction with meat. It can also be used occasionally in place of meat, but exercise caution as it can cause minor stomach upsets.

Och aye from the Highlands

Scottie Oats (Porridge!)

300ml/½ pint/1¼ cups water
pinch of salt
50g/2oz oatmeal or porridge oats

Boil the water in a pan and add the salt and oatmeal or oats gradually, stirring continually. Once all the oats or oatmeal have been stirred in, reduce the heat immediately, and keep stirring as the mixture starts to simmer. Cover and leave simmering gently for a further 10–15 minutes, checking every now and then to ensure the porridge hasn't got too thick (if it has, add a little more water). Allow to cool overnight, and serve for breakfast.

Getting stuck in: all dogs are carnivores, but paying occasional lip service to the omnivore means that whatever you serve, they will be ready to eat it . . .

Mediterranean madness

Almost Veggie

50g/2oz cabbage, cut into strips
50g/2oz carrot, peeled and cut into strips
½ green, red or yellow pepper,
cut into strips
1 small onion, peeled and chopped
2 spring onions, cut into
1cm/½in lengths
1 handful dog biscuits, crumbled
(optional)
30ml/2 tbsp plain yogurt

Put all the vegetables together in a
bowl, adding the dog biscuits if
using. Mix, tip into a dish and pour
the yogurt over. Garnish with dog
biscuits if desired.

Wolf Pie

enough plain pastry to line a small
pie tin and form a lid
50g/2oz unsalted raw peanuts or
cashew nuts, coarsely ground
75g/3oz broccoli or other
green vegetable, coarsely chopped
2–3 button mushrooms, quartered
75g/3oz plain cottage cheese
a little milk

Preheat the oven to the temperature
recommended on the pack of pastry
(or if you prefer to make your own,
follow your usual recipe). Line the
pie tin and cut out the lid. Mix the
nuts and vegetables in a bowl, and
fold in the cottage cheese. Put the
mixture into the pastry case, and
place the lid on top. Use the milk to
bind the edges of the lid with the
sides, and brush a little extra milk on
top. Bake for the time on the pastry
pack, remove, cool and serve.

Pie paradise

Doggie salads for summer

Pooch Pasta

50g/2oz dried pasta shells
50g/2oz cottage cheese
75g/3oz grated Cheddar
(or similar) cheese

Cook the pasta shells for 3–4 minutes
less than you would for yourself:
dogs prefer them *al dente*. Drain off
the water and stir in the cottage
cheese, not mixing too thoroughly.
Allow to cool, then spread out on a
baking tray. Sprinkle the grated
cheese evenly over, and put under a
grill set to the highest temperature.
When the cheese melts, pull out from
under the grill, cool and serve.

Commercial Dog Foods

We all resort to the take-away and can-opener at times, and so it would be unreasonable to expect you to avoid commercial foodstuffs all the time. After all, less time in the kitchen means more quality time on the sofa with your pal, itself a laudable aim. Here is some basic guidance to getting the most out of mass-produced meals.

When you look at the labels, most cans seem to suggest that 99 per cent of dog breeders recommend *their* particular brand for long life, vitality, intelligence and good health. But be selective and discriminating: scrutinize carefully the nutritional information given, and experiment widely with your own dog before deciding which brand you buy and offer.

Weighing up the options: the dilemma we all know so well . . . a bone on the lips, a lifetime on the hips.

How Much?

It's almost impossible to give specific recommendations for the amounts of food your dog requires – variables include size, age, the amount of daily exercise taken, and the individual appetite. But here are some very rough estimates for the sort of intakes, based on canned dog meat, an average adult dog might require:

Toy (up to about 5kg/10lb): 115g/ 4oz canned meat plus 25g/1oz meal
Small (up to about 10kg/20lb): 350g/12oz canned meat plus 100g/ 4oz meal
Medium (up to about 20kg/45lb): 450g/1lb canned meat plus 175g/ 6oz meal
Large (up to about 40kg/90lb): 900g/2lb canned meat plus 275g/ 10oz meal

I'll just have a closer sniff – just to check the flavour, you understand.

Very Large (over 40kg/90lb): It depends on just quite how big the dog is! Calculate the quantities by comparing the dog's weight with the measures for a large dog and multiplying accordingly.

As a general rule, follow the instructions on the can, but remember two important points:
■ Some canned dog foods supply a complete diet without additives, but some don't and in these cases they should be supplemented with meal and/or vegetables.
■ The dog-meat manufacturers are in business to sell dog meat. Although they will not recommend unhealthily large quantities, they will tend to err on the generous side. Start your dog off on three-quarters of the recommended quantity, and see how he fares.

Not Out of a Can

Aside from the special meals you'll undoubtedly want to prepare, there are other commercial foods that don't come in cans. These generally fall into one of two categories:

Dried Foods

These crunchy foods are usually designed to supply your dog's complete dietary requirements – but don't assume this is the case: check the pack carefully. As they have a water content of only 10–12% they are more palatable to a dog if served soaked in water or, even better, gravy: if you want to give your companion the best of both worlds, serve half the quantity dry in one bowl and the other half soaked in another. Milk can be used for the soaking but note that some dogs have difficulty digesting it.

As far as quantities are concerned, consult the instructions on the pack and start your dog off on about three-quarters of the manufacturer's recommended serving.

Always ensure you give your dog plenty of water to complement a serving of dried food.

Semi-moist Foods

These are, once more, generally intended as complete diets – but check the pack to make sure. Usually you can expect to give your dog about one-third of the weight suggested for a canned food. Semi-moist foods contain approximately 20–35% water, while most canned foods provide 75%.

Well . . . one can't hurt, can it? You have to keep your strength up.

TIPS FOR AUGMENTING COMMERCIALLY PRODUCED FOODS
Every chef knows the trick of embellishing canned food and passing it off successfully as home-made. Here are a few tricks for your own kitchen:
■ *Mix in a heaped tablespoon or so (more or less, depending on the size of the serving) of oatmeal, wholemeal breadcrumbs or pulverized breakfast cereal.*
■ *Add any leftover vegetables you have – indeed make it a practice when cooking your own meals to allow for "leftover" vegetables that your dog might like.*
■ *Dog biscuits can be bought inexpensively in huge packs. Although their primary purpose is as treats, throw a few into your dog's bowl each mealtime to add a variation of texture.*
■ *Never forget to offer plenty of fresh water alongside any meal.*

What can beat a home-made treat?

Entertaining

Dogs are by nature extremely gregarious – after all, they have been running with the pack for thousands of years. So occasionally it is a great treat to invite a few of your companion's best friends over – either for an informal "at-home" with party snacks, a more formal dinner, or something livelier. Cooking for a group of dogs shouldn't cause too much anxiety at all. Every one of the recipes included here can be scaled up in bulk without too much effort or extra time consumed. You know that you won't be stuck with any messy leftovers, or too much washing up for that matter, because one or other of your dog's guests will make sure that every last dish is licked clean!

*Everyone loves a party
(and a tail) that goes
with a swing.*

Etiquette

Don't expect too much in the way of table manners and you won't be disappointed! It's a good idea to put each guest's bowl well away from the next: once a dog has firmly understood that the contents of a particular bowl are his or her personal possession, you're unlikely to have squabbles. Of course, once one dog has indicated that he has eaten enough, hungrier dogs may well regard any leftovers as communal property.

If you have a cat among the guests, a little more care is required. To make the feline visitor feel comfortable it is a good idea to serve something that is not available to the dogs: a little milk in a saucer, or perhaps a sardine, is usually perfectly sufficient to subtly indicate that a different species is present while offering a warm and sophisticated paw of friendship.

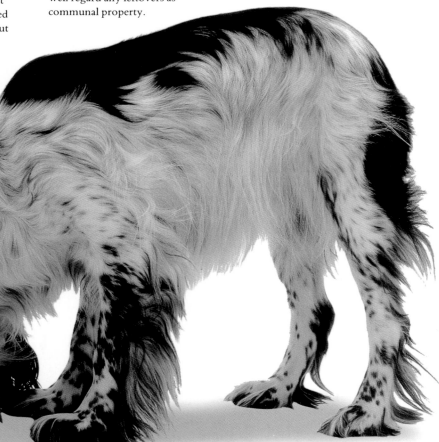

Chunky chicken extravaganza

Grrrrisotto

(quantities are per average-sized dog, as part of a menu)

olive oil
1 potato, peeled and finely chopped
3–4 button mushrooms, cut into quarters
50g/2oz cooked wholegrain rice
50g/2oz canned sweetcorn
75g/3oz cooked chicken, in strips
or chunks
30ml/2 tbsp plain yogurt

Heat the oil, throw in the potato pieces, and sauté until translucent. Add the mushrooms, and keep stirring while adding the rice and the sweetcorn. Next add the chicken, stirring a little longer; reduce the heat to low, and keep stirring for a further 2–3 minutes. Lastly stir in the yogurt, reduce the heat to very low, and continue to stir for 1 more minute. Cover, and leave for 5 minutes, lifting off the lid and stirring briefly every minute or so. Allow to cool completely – overnight is fine – and then serve it up with Sausage Zingers (page 35).

Creamy canine soup

Soup with Happy Tails

(quantities are per average-sized dog, as part of a menu)

½ small can commercial soup –
Cream of Chicken recommended
50g/2oz cooked spaghetti in lengths
of about 8–15cm/3–6in

Heat the soup in a saucepan and mix in the spaghetti. A nice and easy party dish!

DINNER MENU
If you'd like to go the whole dog, why not serve up a de luxe dinner for the occasion with all the trimmings? Here's a suggestion:

POOCH'S PARTY

Appetizer:
Soup with Happy Tails

Entrée:
Grrrrisotto with Sausage Zingers

On the Side:
Almost-Veggie

To Finish:
Raw Carrot

You may not see much of your guests – or one end of them anyway – until the feast is over, but this is usually a sign that they are having a good time.

Doggie Treats

Bones and "Chews"

Chewing on raw (never cooked) bones and picking off little pieces of leftover meat and marrow is very enjoyable, and the gnawing – whether on a real bone or a commercially manufactured "chew" – fulfils the vital function of keeping your dog's teeth healthy, strong and clean. So, though you might be tempted to omit bones from your dog's regular fare because they're messy and can smell, do make an occasional sacrifice.

The best bones are big ones – as big as your dog can sensibly tackle – and smooth ones: reject bones that have sharp or spiky bits, as they can scratch your dog's mouth, which is very sensitive. *Never* give poultry bones – they are too small and brittle and very dangerous.

It is instinctive for dogs to bury bones for storage, so don't become vexed with your friend when you find your herbaceous border has been devastated. With a little compromise and negotiation you can agree with your dog which areas are OK for bone-interment, and which aren't.

Sweets and Other Treats

Commercial sweets for dogs are readily available, and of course your companion will be eager to share any human sweets that are going. Your big responsibility is to keep sweet-giving to a minimum for the sake of your dog's health.

Paws off! I found it, and it's mine.

Getting to grips with an issue: a good bone chew can be a meditative experience.

Sound tips for Dogs 1: never tackle a bone that's bigger than you are.

Sound tips for Dogs 2: hesitate and you've lost it. There's gnaw taste like it . . .

If you can't find a real one . . . a fake will do.

Treat Bag

This personal pooch pouch will enable you to keep your dog's treats out of sight until a reward is deserved.

You will need:

tracing paper • pencil • card • scissors • scrap of material for dog bone • two oblongs of fabric 28 × 40.5cm (11 × 16in) • pins and needle • black cotton thread and thread in a contrasting colour • sewing thread in a matching colour • 0.5m (18in) ribbon

1 From the pattern on page 92 make a template of a dog bone shape and cut it out in the scrap of fabric. On the right side of one of the oblongs of fabric, pin the bone in place. In pencil write your dog's name above the bone.

2 Back stitch over the name with black cotton. Then sew on the bone in another coloured thread. Press.

3 Putting right sides together, pin, tack and sew the two pieces, leaving the top and 6.5cm (2½in) down the sides unsewn.

5 Fold 2.5cm (1in) of the top of the bag down. Pin, tack and sew to create the casing.

6 Finish off the ends, then turn the bag right side out, trimming the corners to get a nice pointed edge. Thread the ribbon through the casing.

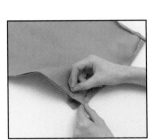

4 Fold 1.25cm (½in) of the top edge to the wrong side and press. Fold in 5mm (¼in) twice on the unsewn parts of all four side seams. Then press.

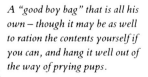

A "good boy bag" that is all his own – though it may be as well to ration the contents yourself if you can, and hang it well out of the way of prying pups.

Decorated Dishes

"As dogs . . . have vivid dreams, and this is shewn by their movements and the sounds uttered, we must admit that they possess some power of imagination. There must be something special, which causes dogs to howl in the night, and especially during moonlight . . ." Charles Darwin, *The Descent of Man*.
We tend to forget that our dogs possess this faculty of imagination – that they are dreamers, and have fantasies, just like us. So don't serve your dog's meals in the same drab old dish every day, but draw on the possible contents of doggie dreams to create something really charming and special, like the ideas shown here.

Your pet may prefer naive realism that evokes days in summer fields . . .

. . . or painted patterns for a more chic effect.

Boney Bowl

This bowl will brighten up any mealtime. Vary the design to suit your dog and make sure you use non-toxic enamel paints.

1 Wash the bowl in the vinegar solution to remove any grease. Dry thoroughly. Draw your design onto the bowl with a chinagraph pencil.

2 Paint on the design then place in a cold domestic oven and bake for 30–45 minutes at 160°C/325°F/Gas 3. Do not remove until cool.

The bones on the outside look almost as good as the bones on the inside.

You will need:

yellow china bowl • 600ml (1pt) warm water with 10ml (2 tsp) vinegar • chinagraph pencil • blue water-based craft enamels (for use on ceramics) • small paintbrush

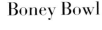

Eurodog Bowl

These bowls, decorated with a portrait of your pooch and his favourite cosmopolitan phrases, will add a continental flavour to feeding time.

You will need:

plain white ceramic dog bowl • 600ml (1pt) warm water with 10ml (2 tsp) vinegar • water-based craft enamels (for use on ceramics): black, blue, yellow and red • fine paintbrush

1 Wash the bowl in vinegar solution. Dry thoroughly. Using the black enamel, paint the dog's outline and features.

2 When dry, paint the collar and dots in blue. Using the yellow and red enamel, paint in more dots.

3 When the bowl is dry, paint your wording around the edge of the bowl using red enamel. Then place the bowl into a cold domestic oven and bake for 30–45 minutes at 160°C/325°F/Gas 3. Do not remove until it has completely cooled.

All well-travelled dogs will appreciate a witty bowl in the language of their friends.

TRANSLATION GUIDE

"Woof Woof": English
"Wau Wau": French
"Ouah Ouah": Italian

Special Occasions

Possibly because your companion is so alert to your own moods, he can always sense when there's a festive occasion in the offing – just like us, he gets excited during the days leading up to it. On the day itself he will expect his share of particular pampering and attention. Such special occasions demand special dishes, so here are a few ideas.

Birthday Boys and Girls

The most important Dog Day of all is of course your pet's birthday, and this is the special occasion he really will have been waiting for. Take the opportunity to dish up all your pet's favourite doggie delights and to pamper him in style.

The ultimate birthday cake in a festive setting. Dog biscuits have been hand-tinted with edible food colouring, and mounted together in an amazing temple structure. The pet's pride is palpable.

My heart belongs to you

Valentine's Day

What food could you serve your dog on Valentine's Day other than heart? You can buy heart-shaped pastry-cutters (metal or plastic), so use them to make a shaped pastry base or toast garnish for a loving meal of:

All My Heart

*½ green, red or orange pepper, finely diced
15ml/1 tbsp lard
75g/3oz beef heart, finely diced
50g/2oz grated cheese*

Fry the pepper in lard for a couple of minutes over a moderate heat in a frying pan. Add the heart and mix well, frying until the meat starts to brown. Put the mixture in a bowl and, while it is still hot, mash in the cheese. Cool and serve.

Easter

Your dog of course may well request an Easter egg for breakfast: not at all good for the general health, but if it happens only once a year it won't do any harm. And for a special supper:

Eggstravaganza

*300ml/½ pint/1¼ cups milk
15ml/1 tbsp icing or caster sugar
3–4 drops vanilla essence
2 egg yolks*

Gently heat the milk, sugar and vanilla essence in a pan until they are just about to boil. Meanwhile, beat the yolks in a bowl. When the hot milk mixture is ready, pour it into the bowl, over the yolks, and stir for about 1 minute. Pour back into the pan and keep stirring until the consistency is a little sticky. Pour into an egg mould and cool.

Springtime special

Fancy festive foodstuffs

Canine Christmas

Your dog will almost certainly want to share your Christmas pudding, whether you want to or not (you will, because he's your friend). One way to forestall his sneak attack on your dessert is to make and serve:

Pooch Pudding

75g/3oz lard
50g/2oz icing or caster sugar
75g/3oz wholemeal breadcrumbs
15–30ml/1–2 tbsp low-sugar
(e.g. diabetic) marmalade
5ml/1 tsp orange juice
1 large egg, beaten

Mix the lard, sugar, breadcrumbs and marmalade together vigorously in a bowl. Add the orange juice and beaten egg and stir well. Put everything in a greased ovenproof bowl and steam for about 2½ hours. Serve cold.

Thanksgiving

At this of all times, turkey surely has to be the order of the day. For a celebration evening meal for your special chum, nothing could be more apposite than:

Turkey Fritters

1–2 eggs, beaten
15ml/1 tbsp milk
15ml/1 tbsp flour
15ml/1 tbsp lard
1–2 palm-sized turkey steaks,
cut from the cooked breast

Beat the egg, milk and flour together to make a batter. Heat the lard in a frying pan over a moderate heat, dip each turkey steak in the batter until evenly coated, then fry until pale golden. Cool to lukewarm, and serve.

Tempting turkey treat

Hair of the dog?

Festive Drinks

Don't ever be tempted to serve your companion alcohol even on festive occasions. The following, however, is something that your friend will enjoy and, later, thank you for with bright eyes and a wagging tail.

Anytime Canine Cocktail

50g/2oz grated carrot
2–3 tomatoes, sliced

Put the ingredients into a blender or food processor and process for about 30 seconds. If the mix looks insufficiently liquid, add a little water and process a little longer. Serve as soon as possible.

Beauty Parlour

Every cute canine likes to look good as a matter of course, and time spent in the bathroom and boudoir is an essential part of the daily regime. This chapter provides invaluable advice on how to create the appropriate setting, with full techniques for perfect pooch presentation and beauty care.

All dogs need to be pampered, and the ultimate wash-and-brush-up guide gives grooming techniques, massage and aromatherapy tips, home beauty parlour treatments and decorative fur stylings. Your dog is already beautiful to you – but he also needs to feel consistently good about himself. This is how to go about it.

The ultimate poodle parlour – this dog is puffed up, preened and ready to go to the party. The beauty regime is a highly significant part of every pampered pet's day, and a sumptuous setting can only enhance the enjoyment.

Fancy fur styles for the long-haired pup – try top-knots, flick backs, braids, beading and bows. If it stays in, your pet loves it.

Wash and Brush-up Guide

We all have our embarrassing personal habits, and one that many dogs share is rolling around in mud, leaves and substances that smell. On such occasions a bath is particularly called for, and even without such an immediate reason, you will want to bathe your friend every month or so, at the very least.

Always use a proper canine shampoo and always ensure that, afterwards, you rinse off every trace as otherwise your dog will suffer itchy skin. Make sure you don't get shampoo in your dog's eyes, mouth or ears. Keep your companion's collar on; he will almost certainly try repeatedly to jump out of the bath, and this will give you something to hold on to.

One thing to watch out for: your dog may immediately want to smother the clean smell with more organic ones by rolling around outdoors. Keep him inside for a few hours until the impulse passes.

A dog in need of a bath.

A pooch pouch in which to keep all that essential grooming equipment.

Beauty Bag

Every dog needs their own vanity case.

You will need:

scissors • pale blue fabric for the bag • needle and matching thread • pink fabric for the base • pins • picot-edged ribbon • gingham fabric for the lining • pompoms • narrower ribbon

2 Cut a circle from the pink fabric. Pin it to the lower edge of the bag. Gather up the thread (from step 1) to fit. Stitch in place.

4 Make the lining following the method in step 1, then sew to the bag.

1 Cut a rectangle from the blue fabric, and fold it in half. With right sides together sew down the sides and sew a line of running stitch along the bottom.

3 Sew a piece of picot-edged ribbon 5cm (2½in) from the top of the bag.

5 Sew the pompoms onto the bag and thread ribbon through the casing.

The Perfect Bath

Dogs may pretend not to like bathing so have someone on hand to help.

You will need:

bristle brush • cotton wool • canine shampoo • towels • hairdrier

1 Brush the knots out of the hair before you bath your dog.

2 Pay particular attention to the ears, which get very matted.

3 Bathe the skin around the eyes using a piece of moistened cotton wool.

4 Plug the ears, then gently bathe in warm water. Rub shampoo well into the skin, massaging as you do this.

5 Rinse thoroughly, making sure that you remove all the shampoo. Remove from the bath and wrap in a warm, soft towel.

The ultimate preened, pampered and powdered pooch.

6 Remove the ear plugs. Use a hairdrier set on warm if your dog has healthy skin, and brush out the hair.

7 Alternatively, your dog may have other ideas of how to dry his hair . . .

Good Grooming

Although they may not show it at first, dogs do love the tactile experience of being groomed. Aim to groom your dog twice a week, and do try to keep to the regime (both of you!). The details of the grooming procedure vary according to the breed and type of dog that lives with you.

Long Coat: Use your fingers and a slicker brush to tease out gently any areas of matted or knotted hair. Don't be tempted to yank at any obstructions: if an entanglement is completely hopeless, cut it away with sharp scissors – but only as a last resort.

Then brush the coat again with a bristle or pin hairbrush. Finally use a wide-toothed comb. Your companion is now ready for any hair-trimming you feel is necessary.

Wiry Coat: In addition to normal grooming, wire-haired dogs should be "stripped" every few months. This can be done with the fingers. Working from head to tail, simply pull on the coat so that any dead hair comes away easily in your hand.

Smooth Coat: Use a rubber brush, working from head to tail to remove dead hair and other debris, then continue the process with a bristle hairbrush. Finally polish the coat with a soft cloth such as a chamois to bring out the shine.

Short Coat: Use a slicker brush to remove any matts or tangles, then work on the coat vigorously with a bristle brush to get rid of dead hair and other debris. You can use a fine-toothed comb for the tail.

THE MANICURE
Toenails will occasionally need clipping. Clip them carefully using special clippers and smooth rough edges with a nail file.

Perfect Grooming

Keep to a regular routine for grooming sessions so your dog will know what to expect. This will relax him and make the experience enjoyable and therapeutic.

You will need:

bristle brush • cloth or chamois leather • coat conditioner • cotton or silk scarf • toothbrush • mirror

1 Work in sequence, the method according to the breed, with the different grades of brushes.

2 Then wipe down with a cloth or chamois leather, or if you are feeling very spoiling, a powder puff.

3 Apply a few drops of coat conditioner, and rub in well.

4 Why not include a dash of *eau de toilette*, if your pooch likes it.

5 Then, a bit of attention with the toothbrush, which should help with the ever-present problem of canine halitosis.

6 Take time to admire your friend and allow him to revel in his smartness (a mirror can profitably be flourished at this stage).

The tools of the trade are as important as the techniques employed, as every true artiste knows. Your dog will select his favourite brush for the occasion.

Fancy Furstyles

Every now and then, perhaps before
a birthday or special occasion, you
will want to treat your dog to a
professional haircut, but in the
interim you can do basic maintenance
yourself. Over time, you will
probably develop highly professional
skills yourself and be able to attempt
the sophisticated looks shown here.

Dogs with short coats require very
little barbering, although you might
want occasionally to trim the hairs on
the tail and legs.

Dogs with longer coats require
rather more attention: trim the long
hair on the hocks and around the feet,
paying particular attention to the
spaces between the toes, where dirt
and debris can all too easily get
trapped.

Reservoir Dog

*A quick trim, back-comb
and a bit of hair gel and
your pet can join any street
gang it wants.*

*Ready to rock . . .
this dog means
business.*

You will need:

comb • scissors • hair gel

1 As with all hairstyles,
start with a thorough
combing. Trim any stray
whiskers, but do not cut
them down too much or you
won't have any hair to style.

2 To achieve a good
mohican effect, back-
comb the hair.

3 Apply hair gel with your
fingers so that the hair
holds its shape.

Posh Ponytail

This fancy top-knot is sassy and stylish, and is guaranteed to turn heads and set tails wagging.

You will need:

elastic band • slicker brush • bristle brush • rollers • ribbon

2 Then set to work with the bristle brush, paying particular attention to the head and under the chin.

3 Work your way down the back and then under the chest.

4 Finish off with the tail; this will be a knotty area.

1 Secure the floppy fringe in an elastic band then start by working all over the coat with the slicker brush.

Simple and quick to achieve in the salon, this look gives instant glamour even on those can't-do-a-thing-with-my-fur days.

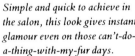

To finish, undo the rollers and gently brush out to form cascading curls around the face. Tie the ponytail with a cheeky ribbon.

5 Be careful as you put the rollers in, so that you don't tweak any of the hairs.

Massage & Aromatherapy

Dogs are very sensitive and tactile creatures – they love being patted, petted, stroked and tickled. So express your love for your dog in a hands-on way by offering a whole body massage. Massage can be combined with the magic of essential oils and scents to bring complete relaxation to your friend.

The Magic of Aromatherapy

For centuries, the pure essences of aromatic plants have been valued for their luxurious scents and their many life-enhancing properties, and your pet will naturally enjoy indulging in the same kind of sybaritic "scentsual" experience as you do.

Your dog will enjoy the beneficial effects of aromatherapy in many ways. Herbal tea bags, if not used for infusions as such, are often appreciated as scented toys in their own right. Fresh growing herbs can be nibbled at or played with. And of course your pet will no doubt appreciate, with you, the more subtle effects of aromatic room burners and scents.

Your dog will no doubt have a very personal response to certain scents, so take these listings very much as a guide, and try out a range of herbs and aromatics until you find a favourite.

Basil A herb for depression and for the lethargic dog.

Bay A possible remedy for sleeplessness (not usually a problem, of course).

Camomile An ideal sedative, as it has a good calming influence.

Cinnamon A useful pick-me-up and general tonic, for sluggish pets.

Eucalyptus Good as a head-clearer, perhaps after a heavy night on the town.

Frankincense Encourages a more meditative state, perhaps appropriate for the more fractious dog.

Jasmine A luxurious flower that will lift the spirits.

Lavender A pleasant tranquillizing scent that will ward off flies and insects.

Marjoram Another herb that will calm and soothe.

Myrrh A great muscle relaxant.

Peppermint Usually used for indigestion, perhaps after a day of over-indulgence.

Pine Good, of course, for breathing difficulties and chills.

Rosemary A good pepping-up herb that will aid concentration and memory – useful for remembering where you keep the slippers for instance.

Sandalwood Used for nervousness and tension, and (if you can face it) an aphrodisiac . . .

The Whole Body Massage

The head-to-toe guide to relaxing your pet.

1 With your friend facing towards you – standing, sitting or reclining – start around the neck area, gently kneading the fur and skin in a rotary motion, pushing in a generally tailward direction.

Important Note:
Remember that essential oils are very powerful and should only be used in highly diluted form and the labels should be followed precisely; don't allow your pet to drink them, and don't use them with pregnant dogs. Essential oils can be wonderful natural remedies, but are never a substitute for veterinary advice if your dog is ill – this list is intended as a light-hearted guide.

2 Progress naturally to the shoulders, rubbing them roughly with the flats of your hands, again with a rotary motion but interspersing this with long strokes towards the rear.

3 At this stage move round to the back. The sides come next; larger dogs will probably appreciate it if you become quite rough with them when buffing the sides vigorously, using the flats of the hands and even the knuckles. The spine itself is sensitive, so be very gentle as you stroke along it from head to tail.

4 Next comes the head: stroke the forehead back from the nose and – if your friend likes it (not all dogs do) – tickle behind the ears and along the jaw.

5 If you want, you can come round to the front again and rub your dog's face with your own – although you may find this difficult in practice because he will undoubtedly by now be trying to rub you back!

The top-to-tail massage, specially adapted for floor practice, will totally relax and rebalance your pet. The restorative power of touch has restored his equilibrium and (once he wakes up) renewed his vitality.

6 Then it is time for the underside, with your dog rolling on the floor as you work on the chest.

7 Around this time – if not before – abandon the plans for a formal massage and just have fun.

Sports,
Games and
Pastimes

Romping is the name of the game as far as dog
sports are concerned, and you probably feel
much the same. Chasing for sticks, splashing in
water, catching frisbees, chewing a rubber ball to
pieces or heading
a football all over
the park – these
are the active ways
by which your
dog adds that
essential spice
to his life.

This energetic
chapter reveals how you can expand your repertoire
of canine sports and range of doggie toys and tricks
to learn, as well as providing invaluable advice on
the perfect dog walk, and creating appropriate
sportive accessories.

The caring owner will encourage a serious sportsdog to meet his full potential, with fulsome praise, support and encouraging rewards.

Try to present your pet with a stimulating range of excitingly different items to chase, jump for and chew . . . though of course the frisbee is a perenially popular stand-by.

Walkin' the Dog

All dogs love "walkies": it is a time when the companionship between you and your dog can be most profoundly felt and expressed.

There are many aspects to consider when planning this crucial activity, and your pet will appreciate your efforts to make it as satisfying as it can be. The trip-round-the-block and late-night-garden-dash are well-tried-and-tested walk techniques, but there are many more methods available in the advanced walk repertoire, and with a bit of practice both you and your pet will soon be superior practitioners of the art.

Entice your pet to accompany you to new and exhilarating locations – hillside, fell, woodland and (for holiday excursions) seaside. Mud, sand, water – all offer new textures and sensations for running through and rolling in.

Apart from the location, the appropriateness of walkwear, both for practical and aesthetic considerations, should never be overlooked. Similarly, you'll need sports equipment, the personal rug for rest moments, the titbits for stamina, and cooling water for quenching the thirst.

Most dogs love swimming in rivers and the sea, and it can be hard to persuade them that it's time to come out of the water. As with a child, don't encourage your dog to go in too deep; keep a close watch, and never ignore beach or lifeguard warnings about swimming conditions.

Don't forget the travelling rug when out and about further afield.

The call of the wild . . . If you live near open land or woodland, your dog and his pals can go romping merrily for hours on end – your favourite hound's dream come true! You will both feel more secure if he carries a name and address label on his collar.

Pit-stop Blanket

If the walk is going to be part of a day out, perhaps with a picnic in the middle of it, your dog will be glad to flop down on this warm travelling rug for a rest or just for a bask in the sun.

You will need:

75cm (30in) square of tartan wool fabric • tracing paper • soft pencil • scissors • fusible bonding web • close-woven black cotton fabric • needle and matching threads • stranded cotton embroidery threads: red, green and blue

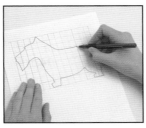

2 Enlarge the template of the dog on page 92. Trace the enlarged dog repeatedly onto the fusible bonding web. Draw half of the dogs facing to the left and half facing to the right.

3 Iron the marked bonding web onto the black fabric and carefully cut out. Peel off the paper backing and position the dogs on the tartan rug. Press on with a hot iron and stitch round all the edges, if necessary.

4 Embroider collars onto some of the dogs and coats onto others. For the collars, sew long threads across the neck of the dog and weave in different colours to create a tartan effect. Use French knots to make "studs" on others. For the coats, sew long diagonal threads across the dog's back in two directions to create a trellis pattern. Use a contrasting colour to trim the edge of the coat and sew tiny cross stitches at each join to hold the threads down.

1 Straighten each side of the tartan material by trimming along a woven thread. Pull out the woven threads to a depth of 2–3cm (¾–1¼in) to make a fringe round all the sides.

A personalized pooch rug ensures that pride is maintained even when frequent recuperation stops need to be made.

Walking Tall

Your pet's pride would be seriously undermined if he felt in any way outdone in the competitive world of kerb-and-field fashion, and you should take great care in the appropriateness and style of that most fundamental canine accoutrement – the lead.

In choosing the lead, there are naturally some practical functions to consider, which may dictate your choice. You may both prefer the intimacy of the short leash, which keeps your dog snugly at your side; then again you may favour the longer version that allows more scope for the well-trained pooch. For those intent on exploration and discovery, the extending model would be the choice, allowing great freedom with the ability to be rewound on the odd occasion when things get out-of-hand.

Long leads, short leads, extending leads, rope leads, chain leads, leather leads . . . The choice can be bewildering. Experiment with your dog and find the type of lead you both prefer.

The extending lead is your pet's preferred style of walkgear, allowing him to feel in full control of the situation.

Simple style conveyed in classic tartan – this collar and lead provide Highland flair for city streets.

An older dog who wants to take things a little quietly while on more gentle strolls will thank you for this heart-warming knitted coat. Things can get cold if you don't walk quickly enough to generate your own heat.

A Barbour-style jacket looks good as your dog trots smartly along beside you in the city streets, but it's also rugged and flexible enough to be the perfect coat for outdoor action.

Doggie Towel

Dogs can dry themselves very quickly by vigorous shaking, but in cold weather do be prepared to help. In any case, the towel offers yet another simple craft opportunity for personalizing one of your dog's favourite belongings.

You will need:

scallop-edged 5cm (2in) even-weave linen band • pins • matching threads • tacking thread and needle • scissors • blue and ivory stranded embroidery cotton • dark blue towel

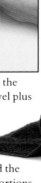

1 Cut a linen band the width of the towel plus 3cm (1½in). Fold in half lengthways and tack along the marked line. Fold the band into six equal portions and tack down each line.

2 Using the tacked thread as a guideline, work embroidered cross stitch with blue and ivory embroidery cotton over two threads of the linen. Following the chart on page 92, sew quarter cross stitch in between by making a tiny diagonal stitch over one thread only.

Lots of water along the route of the walk? Your dog will be glad of this specially made towel – and so will you!

3 Remove the tacking thread and press the band on the wrong side with a damp cloth. Pin the band onto the towel, turning in the ends, and sew invisibly along all the sides.

Dog Delights

Your dog's toys can be as simple or as elaborate as you wish, but certainly there should be some: otherwise he is likely, quite justifiably, to appropriate household objects to chew. For playing outside, a relatively chew-proof rubber ball and a frisbee are standard items, although you can merely use sticks picked up along the way for endless games of fetch. You can also buy in pet shops balls that have bells or squeakers in them (the noise satisfies your companion's predatory instincts), or balls that have asymmetrical shapes – when you throw them they bounce unpredictably, so giving him something *really* interesting to chase. Floating toys are good if you live near open water.

For inside the home you can buy squeaky toys that allow lots of scope for canine contentment, but best of all are chewy "bones", made out of plastic or hide. Gnawing away at one of these gives your companion's jaws good exercise and helps keep the teeth clean.

If your dog persists in chewing your slipper, despite all the alternatives you provide, you might as well give in! There are benefits here in allocating that particular slipper specifically to him as his own property, in order to safeguard all your others.

What a lot of fun can be had with a teddy-bear, particularly if it has a squeak inside. Chew it, snuffle it, carry it and take it to bed . . .

Balls come in all shapes and sizes, so why not give your dog a selection to choose from? He may have a favourite colour (see Your Dog and the Stars), a preferred size or an interest in texture.

Wooden discs on a braided cord offer an interestingly clattery object that your dog will want to leap for again and again. There is an endless variety of toys and play objects that can be created with simple household and craft materials.

The ultimate dog delight – a delicious old boot to chew.

A frisbee is the ideal toy for you and your dog to share when you're out for a walk and a romp in the park. Sometimes canine frisbee-catching competitions are organized; though your friend may not quite aspire to those giddy heights, almost all dogs do become very good at catching frisbees once they've got the hang of the idea. Persuading your dog to give up the frisbee after each catch may prove a little harder to achieve . . .

Tricks and Training

You can't teach an old dog new tricks, or so the saying goes. But in fact you can teach any well-trained dog all number of tricks, if you want to and if you have the patience. Always remember that your dog has a dignity that you should not violate: don't fall into the trap of teaching him tricks that might seem hilarious but are in fact humiliating. And don't forget that the very best tricks your dog will do for you are those that come naturally: watch to see what he already does and build on this.

"Begging" for food or a titbit is another trick that you will find many dogs perform spontaneously. While not to be encouraged at the dinner table, it is nonetheless a sophisticated skill that, in the hands of a master, can draw only admiration. Here we see the classic two-stage technique, with the rear-quiver poise (employing the open-jaw option) moving into the full upright stretch with counterpointing tail and ear.

The perfect "flying leap", like all great acrobatic tricks, looks faultlessly easy to the uninitiated.

Chasing your own tail may look a bit silly to outsiders, but it's good exercise and it can be done almost anywhere . . . and catching a tail is a lot more difficult than you might think!

Shaking paws is an easy trick to teach your friend – indeed, many dogs seem to perform this affectionate action instinctively.

Take a titbit on the nose, flick it high into the air, and then . . . gulp! A clever trick that by no means every dog can master.

Lots of dogs love singing along to music and many of them develop distinct tastes and adopt favourite tunes. Of course, your dog's howling may not seem particularly harmonious to you but then he may feel just the same about your own choral efforts and be too polite to tell you.

Your Dog and the Stars

As your dog curls in the basket or languorously stretches out in front of the fire, the stars may seem a very long way away – but of course they influence your dog's life as much as they do your own. Dog astrology has not yet become a refined science – there are still too many imponderables, notably the difficulty of ascertaining a dog's precise time of birth – but you can make a start in understanding your companion's inscrutable character. The observations in this chapter will enable you to please your pet fully – from selecting favourite foodstuffs to understanding subtle mood swings.

This Libran Alsatian sits knowingly by his scales of justice, amidst the planets. Most Libran dogs possess profound psychic tendencies, but will almost certainly be reluctant to reveal them.

Dogs are fascinated by the stars and planets, and serenade or howl at the moon in moments of deep meditation or contemplation. Like the rest of us, they are asking the universal questions: "Why?"; "How?"; "Who?"; and "When will my dinner be ready?"

Aries
21 March–19 April

Aries dogs are pushers: they are ever-ready to try something new as soon as it occurs to them. Unfortunately, they tend to have little staying power, so very often their ambitious plans come to nothing. They can be tremendous fun to be with, although you have to be prepared to be very tolerant – life with an Aries dog can be extremely rumbustious, so be prepared to say farewell to delicate ornaments and furnishings. Their independent streak can be a nuisance at times, but Aries dogs compensate you for this with their unbounded affection.

Aries dogs are often active, lively and energetic

They have a good appetite which matches their lively attitude to life

Red is the Aries dog's favourite colour

Aries dogs hate to be kept in enclosed spaces

★ *Compatible dogs*: Sagittarius or Leo
★ *Compatible owners*: Leo or Sagittarius
★ *Favourite colour*: red
★ *Lucky number*: 9
★ *Favourite food*: let's just say if it's edible, an Aries dog will usually be happy to eat it, although they favour food they catch when out roaming
★ *Greatest dislike*: being kept for long periods in an enclosed space – Aries dogs are usually natural roamers
★ *Other dog who may share this starsign*: Gnasher (of *The Beano*)
★ *Attributes*: enthusiasm; independence; devotion; fecklessness

Taurus

20 April–20 May

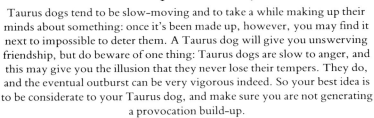

Taurus dogs tend to be slow-moving and to take a while making up their minds about something: once it's been made up, however, you may find it next to impossible to deter them. A Taurus dog will give you unswerving friendship, but do beware of one thing: Taurus dogs are slow to anger, and this may give you the illusion that they never lose their tempers. They do, and the eventual outburst can be very vigorous indeed. So your best idea is to be considerate to your Taurus dog, and make sure you are not generating a provocation build-up.

When roused, Taurus dogs, as symbolized by the bull, can be fiery, difficult and stubborn . . .

Taurus dogs love pastel shades

. . . but Taurus dogs are usually very good-natured and loyal

Taurus dogs have a flair for entertaining their friends in a generous manner, so expect the best meat cuts

★ *Compatible dogs*: Gemini, although be prepared for fights; Libra
★ *Compatible owners*: the natural phlegmatism of a Taurus owner matches well with that of a Taurus dog
★ *Favourite colour*: pastel shades
★ *Lucky number*: 11
★ *Favourite food*: chops

★ *Greatest dislike*: instability of any kind, such as frequent house-moves – although a Taurus dog's fidelity enables it to cope emotionally with most things
★ *Other dog who may share this starsign*: Mr Dogg (of *The Far-Enough Window*)
★ *Attributes*: loyalty; good-nature; temper

Gemini

21 May–21 June

Gemini dogs are usually frisky individuals, and among the most entertaining of all dogs. Their frequent, unpredictable mood changes can be unsettling but, once you are used to them, can be a constant source of pleasure. Gemini dogs are insatiably curious, and will pry into everything, so try to keep them away from valuable items like electronic equipment. Be sensitive to your Gemini dog's moods: just because the animal seems full of *joie de vivre*, don't assume he is unfailingly happy; make sure you check frequently that his physical health is as good as his general bounciness might lead you to think.

Gemini dogs change their mind about most things, including their favourite colour.

The key to the Gemini diet is variety, choice and novelty

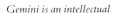

Gemini is an intellectual sign, so don't expect young pups to be enthralled by a simple toy

Geminis are lively, clever, witty and intelligent

★ *Compatible dogs*: Taurus, although be prepared for fights
★ *Compatible owners*: Libra – your commonsense pragmatism makes an excellent counter to a Gemini dog's habitual flightiness
★ *Favourite colour*: yellow
★ *Lucky number*: 3
★ *Favourite food*: almost impossible to predict – Gemini dogs are notorious for going off foods for varying periods of time, so make sure you always have several choices to hand
★ *Greatest dislike*: boredom
★ *Other dog who may share this starsign*: Georgette (of *Oliver & Company*)
★ *Attributes*: curiosity; energy; bounciness; indecisiveness

Cancer

22 June–22 July

Cancer dogs tend to be sensitive creatures and devoted pets so long as you are as sensitive to their moods as they are to yours. A Cancer dog will likely have a strongly developed sense of what is fair and what is not, so be prepared for some early "discussions" as you establish whose territory is whose and what time meals should be served. Do beware of clinging to your Cancer dog only for comfort – when you are upset or unhappy about something – as these animals can pick up your emotions and assume that you do not care for them as much at other times.

Cancer dogs have a penchant for muted tones

Vary the flavours and textures of their food to keep Cancer dogs tempted

Cancer dogs are very emotional and sensitive

Cancer dogs will see off dogs much larger than themselves

★ *Compatible dogs*: Scorpio
★ *Compatible owners*: Scorpio again, although they get on especially well with Aquarians, and (like all dogs) will respond well to a loving owner
★ *Favourite colour*: muted beige, earth tones and other soothing shades
★ *Lucky number*: any number but 13
★ *Favourite food*: mixed, interesting food – Cancer dogs are especially sensitive to different textures, so try to vary the types of meals you offer
★ *Greatest dislike*: any type of emotional violence
★ *Other dog who may share this starsign*: Dogtanian
★ *Attributes*: moral rectitude; sensitivity; strong will; jealousy

Leo

23 July–22 August

Most Leo dogs assume themselves to be the king of the local jungle. If you bring a Leo dog into your home, expect him to be in no doubt as to who is going to be boss! Initially they can seem haughty and unapproachable. Once you have earned the friendship of a Leo dog, however, you have a friend for life. Leos can be difficult with other dogs who are not prepared to be pack-followers; they will regard it as their entitlement that their food be served first, and that the helping be significantly larger. So be prepared for some initial upsets if introducing a Leo dog to others, or *vice versa*.

Being theatrical by nature, Leo dogs love dressing up

Underneath the extrovert personality of the Leo dog lies a good and loyal heart

Leos hate being shown disrespect, which is just what kittens are likely to do

Only the best for Leos, so roast beef is the prime option

★ *Compatible dogs*: Aries or Sagittarius – or another Leo
★ *Compatible owners*: Aries, Taurus, Leo – usually only someone with the same strength of character as a Leo dog can cope!
★ *Favourite colour*: regal red or imperial purple
★ *Lucky number*: 1

★ *Favourite food*: roast beef or smoked salmon
★ *Greatest dislike*: being treated disrespectfully; kittens, young puppies and other scoundrels
★ *Other dog who may share this starsign*: Sirius
★ *Attributes*: entertaining; self-centred; theatrical; responsible

Virgo
23 August–22 September

Virgo dogs tend to be quiet, self-effacing, neat and exact, and may seem to be remarkably cool to your approaches. As a rule they are quite undemonstrative dogs. Don't be misled into thinking that this is a sign of arrogance – far from it, because Virgo dogs, while often highly intelligent, tend habitually to underestimate their own worth and consequently be shy and unable to believe that you are prepared to commit so much of your devotion to them. Once they are convinced that indeed you love them, they will return your love in full measure.

Virgos are reserved towards strangers but they are loyal to those whom they trust

They love chicken, but remember to remove all the bones

Virgos aim for perfection, and are very appearance-conscious

Virgos are reserved towards strangers but they are loyal to those whom they trust

★ *Compatible dogs*: Capricorn
★ *Compatible owners*: any sign – Virgo dogs respond to you as a person rather than to you as a type
★ *Favourite colour*: green and dark brown
★ *Lucky number*: 7, though 6 will do
★ *Favourite food*: no decided preferences, though a general inclination towards blandness might suggest poultry or creamed cod roe
★ *Greatest dislike*: not being loved; any form of emotional insecurity
★ *Other dog who may share this starsign*: Deputy Dawg
★ *Attributes*: sensitive; self-obsessed; reserved; smart

Libra

23 September–23 October

Libran dogs can be charming and sociable, and normally can be persuaded to see things your way. They are often slow to make up their mind but, as with Taurus dogs, once it has been made up it can be hard to change it! They generally get on well with people and with other dogs, and are usually prepared, after a short period for decision-making, to join in wholeheartedly with whatever the rest of the gang has determined to do. Once a Libran dog has decided to trust you, do be aware that you must be worthy of that trust: any betrayal of it would be cruel.

Easy-going and cheerful, Libran dogs like socializing

Libran dogs dislike living alone

Rashers of bacon are a first-choice food for Libran dogs

Libran dogs hate hostile cats

★ *Compatible dogs*: Taurus, Aquarius
★ *Compatible owners*: no special preferences, although Libra dogs do seem to get on particularly well with Sagittarians
★ *Favourite colour*: pink, pale green and blue
★ *Lucky number*: 19
★ *Favourite food*: cauliflower cheese, if available; perhaps a rasher of unsmoked bacon on a Sunday as a special treat
★ *Greatest dislike*: hostile cats; ghosts and ghouls
★ *Other dog who may share this starsign*: Bonzo (of the *Bonzo Dog Band*)
★ *Attributes*: arrogance; sociability; sulkiness; determination

Scorpio

24 October–21 November

Of all dogs, Scorpios are likely to be the most promiscuous – in every sense of the word. They tend to be the most psychologically complicated and interesting of all dogs, although their natural egocentricity can be tiring at times. They give you the outward manifestations of affection easily enough – they will make up to anyone, if they think it is in their interests to do so – but earning their deeper love can require great patience on your part. Once you have done so, however, you could hope for no better companion. No one falls asleep during the Scorpio Show!

Scorpio dogs will make friends with anyone if they think it is in their interests

Sausages are a Scorpio dog's favourite meal

Scorpios have powerful feelings and tend to like strong colours

They work hard and play hard, and dislike being kept on a tight rein

★ *Compatible dogs*: Cancer
★ *Compatible owners*: another Scorpio can be the best bet – if you're a bit emotionally promiscuous yourself, a Scorpio dog might be your ideal pet!
★ *Favourite colour*: deep red and maroon
★ *Lucky number*: 111
★ *Favourite food*: tripe and onions, or alternatively sausages
★ *Greatest dislike*: being kept on the lead too much; not being allowed to roam free
★ *Other dog who may share this starsign*: Pluto
★ *Attributes*: sensitivity; spirituality; intense loyalty; temper and moodiness

Sagittarius

22 November–21 December

Although their characters can sometimes be flawed by over-eagerness – they have a tendency to act first and think afterwards – Sagittarian dogs can be the finest pets of all. They have a certain openness and honesty – even more than other dogs – and they are generally prepared to demonstrate their affection for you, easily won, in a boisterous, good-humoured fashion. Sagittarius is quite a strong sign, so the Sagittarian dog usually gets on well with others and also, notably, with cats. Sagittarian dogs enjoy new experiences: do take care that their natural adventurousness does not lead them into danger.

Sagittarian dogs get on surprisingly well with cats

Sagittarian dogs like strong dark shades of any hue

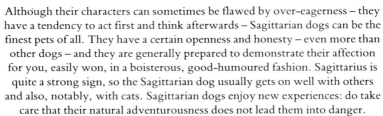

They are generally interested in outdoor sports

They need a constantly varied diet, so give them some fish once in a while

★ *Compatible dogs*: Aries or Leo
★ *Compatible owners*: Aries or Leo
★ *Favourite colour*: rich purples and dark colours
★ *Lucky number*: 22
★ *Favourite food*: the Sagittarian dog's primary food requirement is not a specific dish but a constantly varying, always interesting diet
★ *Greatest dislike*: bureaucrats
★ *Other dog who may share this starsign*: Lassie
★ *Attributes*: intriguing; courageous; superficially reserved; devoted

Capricorn
22 December–19 January

Like their human counterparts, Capricorn dogs usually have the habit of confronting life's obstacles head-on, tending to charge through them rather than try to devise ways of avoiding them; this can be both a strength and a weakness. Despite this gung-ho attitude, they often remain calm in difficult situations, and this has given them the reputation of being callous, calculating dogs. Do not be deceived! A heart of gold lurks within. Capricorn dogs are often addicts of grooming, and you can win them over very easily through plenty of brushing and, perhaps, a ribbon tied with a bow.

Capricorn dogs love being pampered or groomed

They can be rather conventional so they appreciate a classic kennel

Once you get through to your Capricorn dog, you will experience enduring love and loyalty

Treat your Capricorn dog to their favourite poultry once in a while

★ *Compatible dogs*: Virgo
★ *Compatible owners*: Sagittarius, although Capricorn dogs form good bonds with any considerate owner
★ *Favourite colour*: dark green, red, grey, brown and black
★ *Lucky number*: 12
★ *Favourite food*: poultry (do remember to remove all bones), although very adaptable – often fonder of vegetables than most other dogs
★ *Greatest dislike*: television; dogproof fridge doors
★ *Other dog who may share this starsign*: K-9 (of *Doctor Who*)
★ *Attributes*: intriguing; courageous; superficially reserved; devoted

Aquarius
20 January–18 February

Like Scorpio dogs, Aquarian dogs can be psychologically complex, but they lack the broody, dark aspect of the Scorpio dog; this may render them less interesting, but it also makes them a lot easier to live with! They will always approach problems analytically. Gregarious by nature, they can nevertheless reject all companions once they are convinced they are unlikely to get their own way. Many Aquarian dogs have artistic aspirations, so why not set your dog down with a pot of washable, non-toxic paint and a stack of old newspapers and see what happens!

The Aquarian character is kind and friendly but frequently unpredictable

An electric blue castle is perfect for an Aquarian

Aquarian dogs like to stand out from the crowd

Watery, fishy food is ideal for this sign

★ *Compatible dogs*: Libra, Pisces
★ *Compatible owners*: Capricorn, Pisces
★ *Favourite colour*: aquamarine and electric blue
★ *Lucky number*: 8
★ *Favourite food*: water buffalo but, failing this, frogs' legs or gently poached cod
★ *Greatest dislike*: having to pay attention to detail
★ *Other dog who may share this starsign*: Greyfriars Bobby
★ *Attributes*: artistic; mystical; open; individualistic; unpredictable

Pisces
19 February–20 March

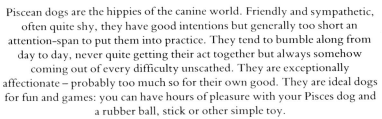

Piscean dogs are the hippies of the canine world. Friendly and sympathetic, often quite shy, they have good intentions but generally too short an attention-span to put them into practice. They tend to bumble along from day to day, never quite getting their act together but always somehow coming out of every difficulty unscathed. They are exceptionally affectionate – probably too much so for their own good. They are ideal dogs for fun and games: you can have hours of pleasure with your Pisces dog and a rubber ball, stick or other simple toy.

Piscean dogs are likely to enjoy competitive games

They love any colour that resembles the sea

Piscean dogs are soft, sensitive and worldly

Why not try a vegetarian dish for your Piscean dog?

★ *Compatible dogs*: Libra, Aquarius
★ *Compatible owners*: no preferences
★ *Favourite colour*: sea green
★ *Lucky number*: 2
★ *Favourite food*: once every few weeks, your Pisces dog might appreciate a dish of wholegrain brown rice as a special treat
★ *Greatest dislike*: Pisces dogs seem to

have no particular detestations, perhaps because they, you know, have difficulty getting it together to, er, dislike *anything*, however ungroovy, baby . . .
★ *Other dog who may share this starsign*: Perdita (of *101 Dalmatians*)
★ *Attributes*: indecisive; genuine; good-spirited; reserved; vague

Special Treats

With such a caring owner as yourself, your dog's life will assuredly be a happy one: lots of attention to health and diet, plenty of exercise, the right amount of spoiling . . . but it could be something even more!

Just as with humans, perks are what distinguish  an exciting and fulfilled life from mere existence. Special toys and rewards are only a part of it: the richest dog life has a good degree of regularity – feeding, for example, should occur at predictable times – and is also filled with variety. Try to make every day a special day for your friend: you'll be amply rewarded by bright eyes, a wagging tail and endless affection.

As if plumped-up, plush cushions scattered in rose petals aren't enough, here I am dreaming of yet more ways you can make a fuss of me. But, as you know, I am worth every effort . . . As in any relationship, little presents and thoughtful gestures are a wonderful way to express affection.

This is my chew: I earned it; I deserve it; and I am going to enjoy every minute of its mastication. Oh, and, by the way, thank you . . . I love you very much too.

Patting, Stroking and Cuddling

Dogs love physical contact – with virtually anything, but especially with you. Never be shy of playing physically with your dog: every time you touch him you are communicating the dedication you feel. A gentle pat on the head or a rougher one on the flanks is a much-appreciated reward for any particular piece of good behaviour, but don't restrict your patting just to those occasions: every second of companionship is worthy of reward.

Although dogs love to be cuddled by their owners, they may take matters into their own hands and give each other a cuddle and a hug too.

Try to make sure there is a regular slot for a cuddling session every day . . . it will have a calming effect on rowdy pups.

Stroke Sequence

Cuddling and stroking is a special time for owners and canines alike. Make time for showing affection – perhaps when you and your friend curl up to watch a favourite television programme.

1 Start a "cuddling" session by patting on the head – much as at the beginning of a formal massage.

2 Work on the head and the ears. The sensation of stroking should feel as good to him as it does to you.

3 If your companion seems receptive to bonding, start moving slowly down the back applying the pressure in even movements.

4 Some dogs particularly like having their chests stroked, and will lift their head to allow for extra long, luxurious strokes.

5 Slow down the movements as he becomes more relaxed.

6 When he is ready for a full-body stroke he will let you know by taking to the floor. Start stroking chest and tummy, slowly at first.

Ready to be stroked. Not all breeds respond well to cuddling and stroking; some are more manly and reserved and prefer to disguise their emotions. But for those that enjoy affection expressed through touch, this is a great delight.

7 Finish off with a vigorous rub that will bring him back to life.

Responding to the Inner Dog

Communication is a two-way process. Your dog can understand your hand-signals, a number of your words and certainly your tone of voice, so shouldn't you try to make an effort to understand something of what he is trying to tell you?

Barking
Some breeds of dog almost never bark, but most dogs will use barks for a variety of purposes – to seek attention, to proclaim excitement, to warn off strangers or other dogs – so learn to interpret your companion's "verbal" language.

Howling
Most people think that howling is a sign of unhappiness or discontent, but this is not always the case. Howling is a way of calling others of the pack, which in this instance means you. In addition, many dogs howl when they hear music: far from being a sign of displeasure, the howling shows they are enjoying the sound and trying to sing along.

Whimpering and Whining
Whimpering and whining can usually be taken as a sign of discontent, although many dogs whine to indicate welcome. Once again, watch your dog carefully to learn which sounds mean what.

The "expectant whine" is clearly distinguished in the vocabulary of otherwise similar-sounding whines by its low, constant level. Almost a hum, it can be maintained for minutes at a time, perhaps interrupted occasionally by the parallel "expectant ear rise" and "isolated tail thump". Mostly seen at the dinner table.

The "full-frontal bark" is usually a series of staccato woof sounds intended to indicate confidence, often as part of power play. Commonly linked with the "bark-worse-than-its bite" sequence, it never lasts long. Treat it with respect and you will please your dog immeasurably.

The strong and silent dog (above) has as much to say, in his way. Do not dismiss his superficial reticence as indicating that he has little to communicate; taciturnity can often be the mark of a thoughtful pet.

The happy-go-lucky pooch (below) has no need for words to make his message clear. All this one needs is a tickle.

Anxious body language easily gives away the more fretful pet (above). The defensive posture of the back half here offsets the seeming openness of the front paws and wide expression.

The dog that has reached a state of equilibrium exudes confidence, self-worth and poised relaxation (below). The tail is alert, the ears ready at your command. This dog knows where he is and where he is going.

DOG'S TIP

If your dog does seem unhappy, a good session of cuddling and tickling will often cheer things up. And don't forget to talk: there are few things more reassuring to a dog than hearing you chat in friendly, obviously relaxed fashion. Even if the words make no impact, the tone of voice will – and the love you feel for the world's finest dog will be amply communicated.

Doggie Gifts

Of course you'll want to give your dog presents and rewards virtually every day of the year. Don't hold back – it is a delightful and easily understood means of communicating pleasure and affection. The best gifts are likely to be the ones you make yourself – designed specifically to celebrate your friendship. To make them truly special, wrap them up in custom-designed paper with an individually crafted gift-tag.

Cross Stitch Sampler

Capture those early puppy days in cross stitch.

You will need:

graph paper • coloured pencils • needlepoint canvas • tacking thread in contrasting colour • scissors • sewing needle • embroidery frame • tapestry needle • stranded cottons in a variety of colours •

Bone Card

We all love to feel special on our birthday – and what better way to make your pet feel proud than hand-crafting him a card.

You will need:

double-sided tape • ribbon • coloured and white card • dog bone biscuit • non-toxic silver spray • PVA glue • glitter glue stick • spray adhesive

The ultimate canine card for a special pal.

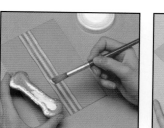

1 Using double-sided tape, stick one ribbon on the coloured card. Spray the bone silver, then when dry glue it onto the card.

2 Leave the card to dry for at least 20 minutes and then decorate further using a glitter glue stick.

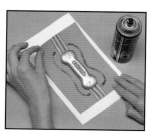

3 Mount the coloured card on a piece of white card and leave to dry.

1 Working from a photo of your dog, draw a portrait onto graph paper.

Immortalize your proud puppy in this personal portrait.

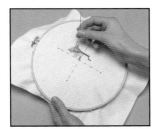

2 Mark the centre of the canvas with coloured thread.

3 Work the sampler in cross stitch.

Sausage-dog Gift Wrap

Wrap your pooch's special gift with this highly decorative wrapping paper.

You will need:

thick paper • acrylic paints: yellow, red, black and green • a range of paintbrushes including a 5cm (2in) flat brush and a fine brush • piece of wood 5cm (2in) thick • thin card • soft pencil • craft knife • tracing paper • PVA glue • gold paste • paper towel

3 Paint the dog and heart red with black high-lights, then before the paint dries use them as printing blocks and print on the stripy paper. Repeat several times.

Your pet will have as much pleasure in unwrapping (ie tearing up and chewing) this specially wrapped gift, as in the contents itself.

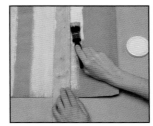

1 Paint thick yellow stripes onto the paper using a flat-headed brush. The stripes should be bold and not too straight-edged. Use a 5cm (2in) piece of wood as a guide rule.

2 Cut a heart out of thin card, then enlarge the template of the dog on page 92, and transfer it onto thin card. Add features to the dog and heart by scoring with the craft knife. Coat with PVA glue and leave to dry.

4 In between each dog and heart, paint the remaining area green. Apply in rough sketchy strokes.

5 To add sparkle, rub gold paste at intervals over the gift wrap with paper towel.

The Perfect Doggie Day

Dear Diary

Yesterday morning the human with whom I share my life let me snooze later than usual. When I was hungry I said so, hinting subtly by batting my bowl around the kitchen floor with my head. Breakfast (no: it was too late for breakfast – let's call it brunch) consisted of Kanine Kedgeree, one of my special favourites. Afterwards I felt a bit full but was eager for a walk nonetheless, so my human took me for a long walk through the woods – where I nearly caught a HUGE rabbit – and along the canal. When we got home I had another snooze, this time next to the radiator and on the lovely new cushion my human has made for me. Whenever I woke up for a moment I had a good chew on my squeaky bone. In the evening Bonzo and Marmaduke came for Festive Biscuits, and afterwards we watched Lassie videos until they had to go home. I was too bloated to do much more than stagger to my basket and sleep. It was a perfect day.

FIDO

Late morning: using Bonzo as a pillow, on a strenuous walk . . .

What a great new ball to chew on.

GOOD MOVIES TO WATCH WITH
YOUR POOCH

A Dog's Life (1918)
Lassie Come Home (1943) and its sequels
Lady and the Tramp (1955)
Old Yeller (1957)
A Dog of Flanders (1959)
Greyfriars Bobby (1960)
101 Dalmations (1961; 1996)
The Incredible Journey (1963)
Benji (1974)
Won-Ton-Ton, the Dog Who Saved
Hollywood (1976)
The Fox and the Hound (1981)
K-9 (1989)
Turner & Hooch (1989)
Beethoven (1992)
Eight Below (2006)
Bolt (2008)
Marley & Me (2008)
Hachi: A Dog's Tale (2009)

Great! Chase-and-chew-the-lead, my favourite game.

Festive Biscuits

To make your dog's day, invite his or her friends to tea and serve up these delicious biscuits.

225g/8oz plain wholemeal flour
225g/8oz sausagemeat
50–120ml/2–4 fl oz water

2 Add enough water to form a soft dough. Turn out onto a floured surface and roll out to approximately 5mm (¼in) thick.

1 Preheat the oven to 350°F/180°C/Gas 4. Mix the flour and the sausagemeat together thoroughly.

Well, it's dinner time – hurry up!

3 Cut out the biscuits and bake in the oven until crispy and golden. Allow to cool and then store in an airtight container.

Perfect for TV snacking: star-shaped sausage cookies.

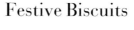

Templates

You can either use the templates the same size as they are reproduced here or enlarge them. To use the same size, simply trace them, transfer onto paper and cut them out. To enlarge, either use a grid system or a photocopier. For the grid method, trace the template and draw a grid of evenly-spaced squares over your tracing. To scale up, draw a larger grid onto another piece of paper. Copy the outline onto the second grid by taking each square individually and drawing the relevant part of the outline in the larger square. Finally, draw over the lines to make sure they are continuous.

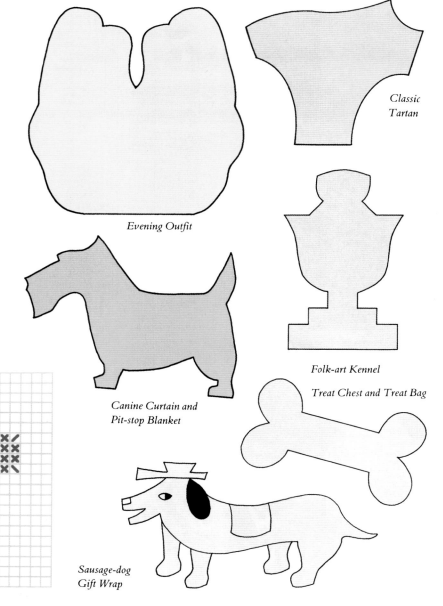

Classic Tartan

Evening Outfit

Folk-art Kennel

Treat Chest and Treat Bag

Doggie Towel

Canine Curtain and Pit-stop Blanket

Sausage-dog Gift Wrap

Knitting Patterns

Abbreviations

K	knit
P	purl
st/s	stitches
tog	together
T	turquoise yarn
Pi	pink yarn

Tension

*18 sts x 22 rows to 10 x 10cm
(4 x 4in) (stocking stitch)*

Winter Woolly

Using red yarn, cast on 60 sts
Rows 1 to 4: K 1, P 1 rib
Rows 5 and 6: K
Row 7: K 8, cast off 14 sts, K 16, cast off 14 sts, K 8
Row 8: K 8, turn knitting round and cast back on 14 sts, turn knitting back round, K 16, turn knitting round, cast back on 14 sts, turn knitting back round, K 8
Row 9: K 7, K 2 tog, K 13, K 2 tog, K 13, K 2 tog, K 13, K 2 tog, K 6 (56 sts)
Row 10: K
Row 11: K 6, K 2 tog, K 12, K 2 tog, K 12, K 2 tog, K 12, K 2 tog, K 6 (52 sts)
Rows 12, 13 and 14: K
Row 15: K 5, K 2 tog, K 11, K 2 tog, K 11, K 2 tog, K 11, K 2 tog, K 6 (48 sts)
Rows 16, 17 and 18: K
Row 19: K 4, K 2 tog, K 10, K 2 tog, K 10, K 2 tog, K 10, K 2 tog, K 6 (44 sts)
Rows 20, 21 and 22: K
Row 23: K 3, K 2 tog, K 9, K 2 tog, K 9, K 2 tog, K 9, K 2 tog, K 6 (40 sts)
Rows 24, 25 and 26: K
Row 27: K 2, K 2 tog, K 8, K 2 tog, K 8, K 2 tog, K 8, K 2 tog, K 6 (36 sts)
Rows 28, 29 and 30: K
Row 31: K 1, K 2 tog, K 7, K 2 tog, K 7, K 2 tog, K 7, K 2 tog, K 6 (32 sts)
Rows 32, 33 and 34: K
Row 35: K 2 tog, K 6, K 2 tog, K 6, K 2 tog, K 6, K 2 tog, K 6 (28 sts)
Row 36: K
Cut yarn and thread through remaining sts to finish off

Knitted Coat

(length 40cm/16in)

Using turquoise yarn, cast on 58 sts
Row 1: K
Row 2: cast on 1 st, K, cast on 1 st (60 sts)
Row 3: K
Row 4: K
Row 5: K 3, P 54, K 3
Row 6: K
Row 7: K 3, P 54, K 3
Start to work in intarsia
Row 8: K 11 T, K 5 Pi, K 44 T
Row 9: K 3 T, P 39 T, P 9 Pi, P 6 T, K 3 T
Row 10: K 8 T, K 11 Pi, K 41 T
Row 11: K 3 T, P 37 T, P 12 Pi, P 5 T, K 3 T
Row 12: K 7 T, K 14 Pi, K 39 T
Row 13: K 3 T, P 36 T, P 14 Pi, P 4 T, K 3 T
Row 14: K 6 T, K 16 Pi, K 38 T
Row 15: K 3 T, P 35 T, P 16 Pi, P 3 T, K 3 T
Row 16: K 6 T, K 17 Pi, K 37 T
Row 17: K 3 T, P 34 T, P 18 Pi, P 2 T, K 3 T
Row 18: K 5 T, K 18 Pi, K 37 T
Row 19: K 3 T, P 35 T, P 17 Pi, P 2 T, K 3 T
Row 20: K 5 T, K 17 Pi, K 38 T
Row 21: K 3 T, P 36 T, P 17 Pi, P 1 T, K 3 T
Row 22: K 4 T, K 17 Pi, K 39 T
Row 23: K 3 T, P 37 T, P 16 Pi, P 1 T, K 3 T
Row 24: K 4 T, K 16 Pi, K 39 T
Row 25: K 3 T, P 37 T, P 16 Pi, P 1 T, K 3 T
Row 26: K 4 T, K 15 Pi, K 41 T
Row 27: K 3 T, P 38 T, P 15 Pi, P 1 T, K 3 T
Row 28: K 4 T, K 15 Pi, K 41 T
Row 29: K 3 T, P 39 T, P 14 Pi, P 1 T, K 3 T
Row 30: K 4 T, K 14 Pi, K 42 T
Row 31: K 3 T, P 39 T, P 14 Pi, P 1 T, K 3 T
Row 32: K 4 T, K 15 Pi, K 41 T
Row 33: K 3 T, P 38 T, P 15 Pi, P 1 T, K 3 T
Row 34: K 5 T, K 14 Pi, K 41 T
Row 35: K 3 T, P 37 T, P 15 Pi, P 2 T, K 3 T
Row 36: K 5 T, K 15 Pi, K 40 T
Row 37: K 3 T, P 36 T, P 15 Pi, P 3 T, K 3 T
Row 38: K 6 T, K 15 Pi, K 39 T
Row 39: K 3 T, P 36 T, P 14 Pi, P 4 T, K 3 T
Row 40: K 7 T, K 13 Pi, K 40 T
Row 41: K 3 T, P 37 T, P 12 Pi, P 5 T, K 3 T
Row 42: K 10 T, K 9 Pi, K 41 T
Row 43: K 3 T, P 39 T, P 6 Pi, P 9 T, K 3 T
Continue with turquoise yarn
Row 44: K
Row 45: K 3, P 54, K 3
Rows 46 to 51: repeat rows 44 and 45 three times
Row 52: K 2 tog, K 56, K 2 tog (58 sts)
Row 53: K 3, P 52, K 3
Row 54: K 2 tog, K 54, K 2 tog (56 sts)
Row 55: k 2 tog, K 2, P 48, K 2, K 2 tog (54 sts)
Row 56: K 2 tog, K 50, K 2 tog (52 sts)
Row 57: K 2 tog, K 2, P 44, K 2, K 2 tog (50 sts)
Row 58: K 2 tog, K 46, K 2 tog (48 sts)
Row 59: K 3, P 42, K 3
Row 60: K 2 tog, K 44, K 2 tog (46 sts)
Row 61: K 3, P 40, K 3
Row 62: K 2 tog, K 42, K 2 tog (44 sts)
Row 63: K 3, P 38, K 3
Row 64: K 2 tog, K 40, K 2 tog (42 sts)
Row 65: K 3, P 36, K 3
Row 66: K 2 tog, K 38, K 2 tog (40 sts)
Row 67: K 3, P 34, K 3
Row 68: K 2 tog, K 36, K 2 tog (38 sts)
Row 69: K 3, P 32, K 3
Row 70: K 2 tog, K 34, K 2 tog (36 sts)
Row 71: K 3, P 30, K 3
Row 72: K
Rows 73 to 76: repeat rows 71 and 72 twice
Row 77: K3, P 30, K 3
Row 78: cast on 18 sts at the beginning of the row, K across the 54 sts on the needle
Row 79: cast on 18 sts at the beginning of the row, K across the 72 sts on the needle
Rows 80 and 81: K
To make the buttonholes:
Row 82: K 66, cast off 3 sts, K 3
Row 83: K 3, turn knitting and cast back on 3 sts, turn knitting back round, K 66
Rows 84 and 85: K
Row 87: K 66 sts, cast off 3 sts, K 3
Row 88: K 3, turn knitting and cast back on 3 sts, turn knitting back round, K 66
Rows 89 to 91: K
Cast off

Stomach strap

Using the turquoise yarn, cast on 7 sts
Rows 1 and 2: K
To make the buttonholes:
Row 3: K 2, cast off 3 sts, K 2
Row 4: K 2, turn knitting round and cast back on 3 sts, turn knitting back round, K 2
Continue knitting until the strap fits round your dog's stomach
To make the buttonholes at the other end of the strap, repeat rows 3 and 4 K 2 rows
Cast off

Basic Sewing Techniques

Tacking

Tacking

This is a temporary stitch used to hold seams together before sewing. The stitches should be between 5mm (¼in) and 1cm (⅜in) long.

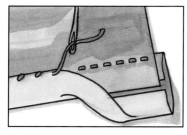

Applying Bias Binding

Applying Bias Binding

Pin the bias binding on the right side of the fabric with right sides facing and raw edges aligning. Tack and machine-stitch in position along the raw edges with a 5mm (¼in) seam allowance. Remove the tacking stitches, turn the free edge of the binding over to the wrong side of the fabric and turn it under itself to create a clean edge. Slip stitch with matching thread to secure in place.

Machine Appliqué

Machine Appliqué

Machine appliqué is quick and hardwearing. Cut out the motif, then pin and tack in position on the main fabric. Set the sewing machine to a close zig zag or satin stitch and sew around the edges of the shape so that the raw edges are covered completely.

Quilting

To achieve good results, the layers of fabric you are working with – usually top fabric, wadding and backing – need to be secured together before you begin. This will prevent the layers from slipping out of position. To do this, lay the backing fabric wrong side up on a flat, hard surface such as a table. Lay the other two layers over the top, ending with the top fabric, right side up, and secure them with tape. Pin, then tack the layers together. For small pieces you can use safety pins instead.

You can then either machine- or hand-sew the quilt. For quilting by hand, work the design using small evenly spaced running stitches. If quilting by machine, a "walking foot" fitted to your machine will help prevent the fabric layers moving and causing puckering.

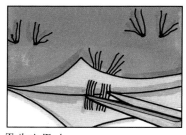

Tailor's Tacks

Tailor's Tacks

This is the most accurate way to transfer markings from a paper pattern onto fabric. With the pattern still pinned in place, make a tiny slit across the symbol to be marked. Using a double thread, tack several loops through both layers. Remove the pattern, gently ease the fabric apart, and cut the loops. The tufts remain in the fabric.